PENGUIN BOOKS

# Gods of Metal

Eric Schlosser is the author of *Fast Food Nation*, *Reefer Madness*, and *Command and Control*, as well as the co-author of a children's book, *Chew on This*. Two of his plays, *Americans* and *We the People*, have been produced in London. He was an executive producer of the films *Fast Food Nation* and *There Will Be Blood*. He was a co-producer of the documentary *Food Inc.*, an executive producer of *Food Chains* and *Hanna Ranch*.

ERIC SCHLOSSER

# Gods of Metal

PENGUIN BOOKS

PENGUIN BOOKS

UK | USA | Canada | Ireland | Australia
India | New Zealand | South Africa

Penguin Books is part of the Penguin Random House group of companies
whose addresses can be found at global.penguinrandomhouse.com.

Initially published as 'Break-In at Y-12' in *The New Yorker*, March 9, 2015 issue
This revised version published in Penguin Books 2015

001

Copyright © Eric Schlosser, 2015

Set in 10.6/16 pt Swift
Typeset by Jouve (UK), Milton Keynes
Printed in Great Britain by Clays Ltd, St Ives plc

A CIP catalogue record for this book is available from the British Library

ISBN: 978-0-141-98226-7

The Y-12 National Security Complex sits amid a narrow valley, surrounded by wooded hills, in the city of Oak Ridge, Tennessee. Y-12 and Oak Ridge were built secretly, within about two years, as part of the Manhattan Project, America's crash programme to create an atomic bomb, and their existence wasn't publicly acknowledged until the end of the Second World War. By then, the secret city had a population of 75,000. Few of its residents had been allowed to know what was being done at the military site, which included one of the largest buildings in the world. Y-12 processed the uranium used in Little Boy, the atomic bomb that destroyed Hiroshima. Seven decades later, Y-12 is still the only industrial complex in the United States devoted to the fabrication and storage of weapons-grade uranium. Every nuclear warhead and bomb in the American arsenal contains uranium from Y-12.

Strict security measures have been adopted at the site to prevent the theft of its special nuclear materials. Y-12 has some five hundred security officers authorized to use lethal force within its Protected Area, five BearCat armoured vehicles, Gatling guns that can fire up to fifty rounds per second and shoot down aircraft, video cameras, motion detectors, four perimeter fences, and rows of dragon's teeth – low, pyramid-shaped blocks of concrete that can rip the axles off approaching vehicles and bring them to a dead stop. The management of Y-12 calls the place 'the Fort Knox of Uranium'.

After the terrorist attacks on September 11, 2001, the Highly Enriched Uranium Materials Facility was built, at a cost of more than half a billion dollars, to safeguard Y-12's uranium. Situated at the north end of the Protected Area, the storage facility is an imposing white structure, longer than a football field, with guard towers at all four corners. If the tops of the towers were crenellated, the building would look like an immense, windowless White Castle. Some 900,000 pounds of weapons-grade uranium are stored inside it. Little Boy – a crude and highly inefficient atomic bomb, designed in the early 1940s with slide rules – contained about 140 pounds of weapons-grade uranium, and almost 99 per cent of it harmlessly blew apart as the bomb detonated. And, when that happened, two-thirds of the buildings in the city were destroyed and perhaps 80,000 civilians were killed. The amount of weapons-grade uranium needed to build a terrorist bomb with a similar explosive force could fit inside a small gym bag.

At about half past two in the morning on 28 July 2012, three people were dropped off at the Scarboro Church of Christ, a modest brick building with a single white spire in an African-American neighbourhood of Oak Ridge. They walked across the church parking lot, made their way through a stand of trees, reached a meadow, and turned left. Up ahead, in the darkness, they could see the silhouette of a steep hill called Pine Ridge. On the other side of the hill was Y-12. All three had spent time in federal prison. They belonged to a loosely organized group whose members have been prosecuted by the Justice Department for violent crimes, sabotage, and threatening national security. The three hoped to reach the uranium-storage facility before sunrise, having carefully planned the intrusion for more than a year. But they had no desire to steal anything or make a bomb. They wanted to 'heal' and 'transform' the building with their own blood; to mark it as a symbol of evil, empire, and war; to protest against its role in maintaining America's nuclear arsenal. Gregory Boertje-Obed was a Christian pacifist in his late fifties who painted houses for a living and worked with the homeless in Duluth, Minnesota. Michael Walli was a Catholic layman in his early sixties, inspired by the life of St Francis of Assisi to live humbly and serve the poor. And Megan Rice was an eighty-two-year-old nun, a member of the Society of the Holy Child Jesus. Carrying flashlights and backpacks, they headed towards the hill.

Not so long ago, the threat of nuclear terrorism seemed imminent. In the autumn of 2001, during an interview with a Pakistani journalist, Osama bin Laden claimed to possess nuclear weapons, and President George W. Bush's administration invoked the prospect of mushroom clouds rising above American cities to justify its wars in Afghanistan and Iraq. 'We judge that there is a high probability that Al Qaeda will attempt an attack using a CBRN' – chemical, biological, radiological or nuclear – 'weapon within the next two years,' John Negroponte, Bush's Ambassador to the United Nations, informed the Security Council in April 2003. 'There is little doubt that Al Qaeda intends to and can detonate a weapon of mass destruction on US soil,' members of a bipartisan commission on national security wrote the following year.

More than a decade later, a nuclear-weapons catastrophe has not yet occurred. The threat has been dismissed as 'alarmist' by some academics and no longer inspires much public concern. But since the early 1980s, a small group of peace activists, devout supporters of the Plowshares movement, have been trying to break into nuclear-weapons sites throughout the United States. They've almost always succeeded. Plowshares actions have not only revealed serious vulnerabilities in the security of America's nuclear enterprise, they've also shed light on the inherent risks faced by every nation that possesses weapons of mass destruction. Having these weapons creates endless opportunities for theft or misuse. At the moment, the probability of terrorists staging a successful nuclear attack may be low, but the consequences would be unimaginably high. And, as Plowshares activists have demonstrated again and again, improbable things happen all the time.

love your enemies

The origins of the Plowshares movement can be traced to the work of Dorothy Day. At the age of eighteen, Day dropped out of college in Illinois and moved to New York City. She was an aspiring writer, a free spirit drawn to the radical politics and bohemia of Greenwich Village in 1916. She soon had a job as a reporter with *The Call*, a socialist newspaper, covering protest marches, strikes, and the birth-control movement. Her family was conservative and Episcopalian, but Day rejected all the trappings of middle-class respectability. She lived in a communal apartment, took lovers, spent time with anarchists and communists, with John Dos Passos, Eugene O'Neill, and John Reed.

By the time Day was twenty-four, she'd been arrested outside the White House while demanding the vote for women and sent to jail for a month; worked as an assistant managing editor at *The Masses*, a left-wing monthly that was shut down after opposing the draft and the First World War; got arrested during the raid of an Industrial Workers of the World flophouse and mistakenly been charged with prostitution; worked as a library clerk, a restaurant cashier, an artist's model, a nurse; had an illegal abortion; gotten married and sought a divorce; moved to Europe and lived on the island of Capri for six months; interviewed Leon Trotsky; and decided to write a novel. After selling the film rights to her first book, she bought a beach house on Staten Island and had a daughter with a common-law husband. And then Dorothy Day did something so radical that few of her radical friends could comprehend it. She became a Catholic. She took a vow of poverty. And she devoted the rest of her life to the practice of a new kind of American

Catholicism – one that was uncompromising in its service to the homeless, its opposition to state power, its resistance to all forms of violence and war.

Dorothy Day sought to emulate Jesus and live the Gospel, embracing a Christianity true to its historical roots. She was greatly influenced by Peter Maurin, a French peasant who'd travelled widely in the United States, taking odd jobs and giving speeches about Catholic social justice. While her downtown contemporaries looked to Marx and Engels for guidance, Day now regarded the Sermon on the Mount as her manifesto: Care little about material possessions or food. Love your enemies, do good to those who hate you, pray for those who persecute you. Blessed are the meek and the peacemakers. In 1933, Day and Maurin founded the *Catholic Worker*, a monthly newspaper that sold for a penny. It published the sort of advocacy journalism that Day had written for years, now imbued with a biblical perspective. The print run of the first edition was about 2,500, and she sold copies of it on May Day in Union Square. The paper's critique of capitalism and defence of labour fit the popular mood at the height of the Great Depression. By the late 1930s, the *Catholic Worker* had a circulation of about 200,000.

No longer content simply to advocate on behalf of the dispossessed, Day and Maurin opened a 'house of hospitality' on Charles Street, in the West Village. It fed and housed the poor, as well as Day and fellow Catholic Workers. Like Jesus, she'd decided to live with 'the rejected ones, the scorned ones', convinced that 'the more luxurious our lives, the further we are from Him'. About thirty hospitality houses soon opened nationwide, along with rural communes that embodied the growing movement's ideal of decentralized power and self-sufficiency. Day no longer cared for socialism or communism. She'd become an anarchist – but preferred the term libertarian, not wanting to offend. She opposed most of the New Deal, believed in changing the world through 'direct action', and never voted in an election.

When the United States entered the Second World War, Dorothy Day urged young men to oppose the war and avoid the draft. Day had little use for traditional Catholic teachings about the morality of armed conflict. She thought there was no such thing as a 'just war'. All wars were sinful, she argued, and a true Christian should be willing to shed one's own blood before taking the life of another human being. Her pacifism alienated many close friends and supporters. Turning the other cheek seemed dangerous, immoral, and ludicrous, at a time when Nazi Germany was massacring civilians. But Day would not budge. She didn't care if her views appeared 'impractical'. They were based on the teachings of the early Christian church, and she vowed to live her faith without compromise, however reckless that might seem. The *Catholic Worker* lost three-quarters of its circulation during the Second World War, and more than half of the hospitality houses closed.

By the late 1940s, America's growing anxiety about nuclear weapons revived interest in Day's pacifism. She had condemned the use of atomic bombs against Japan, calling it a 'colossal slaughter of the innocents'. The possibility of a nuclear war between the United States and the Soviet Union gave new urgency to a movement seeking to make war obsolete. Day admired Mahatma Gandhi and adopted his tactics of non-violent resistance. In 1955, she refused to enter a fallout shelter during a civil-defence exercise in New York City, faced prosecution for breaking the law, pleaded guilty, and called the protest 'an act of penance' for the destruction of Hiroshima and Nagasaki. Her punishment was a suspended sentence. Over the next four years, Day was jailed three times for refusing to participate in the city's annual air-raid drills.

'BAN THE BOMB . . . God is our father, and all men are our brothers,' one of her handouts said. 'We are willing to die for this belief.'

Members of the Catholic Worker movement were among the first Americans to protest the Vietnam War. On 6 November 1965, Day gave a speech at a rally in Union Square, urging young men to burn their draft cards and refuse to serve in Vietnam. A federal law had recently been passed threatening a five-year prison sentence to anyone who tampered with a draft card 'in any manner'. At the Union Square rally, a handful of pacifists, neatly dressed in suits and ties, set their cards on fire, as nearby counterdemonstrators carried signs saying 'Burn Yourselves Instead of Your Cards' and 'Thanks Pinkos, Queers, Cowards, Draft Dodgers – Mao Tse-tung & Ho Chi Minh'. Day told the crowd that being arrested and imprisoned would be an honour, that everyone facing conscription should 'heed the still small voice' of their consciences and 'refuse to participate in the immorality of war'. The speech could barely be heard, as hecklers shouted at Day and called her 'Moscow Mary'. The escalation of the war in Vietnam made Day's form of non-violent resistance seem increasingly quaint and irrelevant. Many of her young followers now thought that a stronger dose of direct action was necessary.

killing is disorder

In the autumn of 1967, Philip Berrigan, a priest who frequently wrote for the *Catholic Worker*, went to the Baltimore Custom House with three other protesters, walked into the draft board, pulled open filing cabinets, and poured bottles of their blood over draft records. While awaiting the legal resolution of that case, he and his older brother, the poet Daniel Berrigan, who was also a Catholic priest, turned the level of non-violent resistance up a few notches. On 17 May 1968, the Berrigans and seven other activists entered a Selective Service office in Catonsville, Maryland. After a brief scuffle with two women clerks, the group grabbed hundreds of draft files from cabinets, carried them into a car park, and set them on fire with homemade napalm. Newspaper reporters and a television crew had been notified of the protest in advance. 'We destroy these draft records not only because they exploit our young men,' a handout given to reporters said, 'but because they represent misplaced power concentrated in the ruling class of America.' The recipe for napalm – a mixture of gasoline and soap flakes – had been found in a Green Beret handbook.

The actions of the Catonsville Nine elevated the

Berrigan brothers to the pantheon of countercul-
ture heroes. In a year that saw the assassinations of
Robert F. Kennedy and Martin Luther King, Jr, riots
in Paris, riots at the Democratic convention in
Chicago, and the Tet Offensive in Vietnam, the spec-
tacle of Catholic priests destroying government
documents with napalm oddly seemed to make
sense. The Berrigans had been raised during the
Depression, amid rural poverty in upstate New
York. Their father was angry and domineering, a
socialist who farmed land owned by the church;
their mother, loving and kind. The *Catholic Worker*
and its values were an integral part of the Berrigan
household. Daniel Berrigan had a shy, poetic
nature. Philip was tall, boisterous, and athletic.
While Daniel studied to become a Jesuit, Philip was
drafted into the army and served as an artilleryman
in Germany and France during the Second World
War. He was haunted for the rest of his life by
images of the bloodshed and the bombed-out cities
in Europe.

Philip Berrigan later attended Holy Cross, joined
the Josephite Fathers and Brothers, a Catholic order
formed to help the African-American community,
and lived in New Orleans for six years, teaching at
an all-black school. Daniel travelled to France and
spent time there with radical 'worker priests' who

left the pulpit to walk picket lines and toil in the fields. The Berrigans became active in the civil rights movement and marched in Selma, Alabama, with Martin Luther King. Their efforts to end poverty, racism, and militarism coalesced into direct action against the Vietnam War. They supported the overthrow of the American-backed South Vietnamese Government, and Philip Berrigan even considered going there and fighting alongside the Vietcong. But he'd sworn, after the Second World War, never to pick up a gun again.

The trial of the Catonsville Nine became a media circus. Thousands of demonstrators marched through Baltimore to support the defendants, and hundreds of anti-war activists waited in line every morning for a seat in court. Philip Berrigan had already been sentenced to six years in federal prison for the customs house case. 'You have transcended the tolerable limits of civil disobedience,' the judge said, justifying that punishment. 'You deliberately set out to use violent means to destroy the very fabric of society.' During the Catonsville trial, Judge Roszel C. Thomsen allowed the Berrigans to discuss their motives on the witness stand, to tell the jury why the war in Vietnam was immoral, to explain why the foreign policy of the United States was illegal, not the burning of draft records. 'We say: killing is disorder; life and gentleness and community and unselfishness is the only order we recognize,' Daniel Berrigan told the court. He later adapted the transcripts of the trial into a play, composed in free verse, that was widely performed and made into a film by Gregory Peck.

Dorothy Day supported the Berrigans but felt uneasy about their form of direct action. It was one thing to burn your own draft card, quite another to burn someone else's. In 1970, after being found guilty in the Catonsville Nine trial, the Berrigans strayed further from her notions of non-violent resistance by going on the run instead of reporting for prison. As a fugitive, Daniel arrived at Cornell University on a motorcycle, gave a speech before thousands of students, and left campus with his head hidden inside the head of a Bread and Puppet Theater puppet. Philip went into hiding with help from Elizabeth McAlister, a nun whom he'd secretly married the previous year. The Berrigan brothers were soon captured and imprisoned. But their war with the government had not ended. While behind bars, Philip Berrigan was indicted, along with McAlister, for conspiring to blow up the steam tunnels beneath federal buildings in Washington DC – and for plotting to kidnap Henry Kissinger, who was President Nixon's national-security advisor at the time. The case against Berrigan and McAlister ended in a mistrial.

When Philip Berrigan was released from the Federal Correctional Institution, Danbury, in December 1972, a large crowd of supporters awaited him at the prison gate. But the national mood had changed during the two years he'd been away. As the war in Vietnam wound down, so did the movement to oppose it. Once featured on the cover of *Time* magazine, Berrigan found that his latest acts of resistance, such as depositing broken and bloody dolls on the White House lawn, attracted little media interest. Now openly married and excommunicated by the Catholic Church, Berrigan and McAlister helped to organize half a dozen 'resistance communities' on the East Coast. Berrigan thought that 'some of us would have to accept God's Word as a handbook and try to embody it'. Only one of the communes – Jonah House, in inner-city Baltimore – lasted beyond the 1970s. And it got off to a rough start. Determined to live outside the capitalist system, members of Jonah House sometimes obtained food by dumpster-diving and theft. Berrigan was arrested at a grocery store for shoplifting, McAlister at a Sears, Roebuck for trying to steal tools. Chastened and embarrassed by the arrests, Berrigan started to work as a house painter.

## hammers and blood

The threat posed by nuclear weapons soon became the focus of Jonah House's activities. As a young second lieutenant training for the invasion of Japan, Philip Berrigan had felt grateful to President Harry Truman for ending the war with two atomic bombs. Now Berrigan saw these weapons as symbols of 'the violence and criminality of the American empire', as a profound threat to all of God's creation. Members of Jonah House carried mock-ups of atomic bombs to the Capitol Building, accompanied by someone dressed as the Grim Reaper. They poured blood on the Pentagon, dug a symbolic grave on the lawn of Secretary of Defense Donald Rumsfeld's house, disrupted services at President Jimmy Carter's church. They went back and forth from Jonah House to jail and looked after one another's children. Berrigan and McAlister eventually had three kids, dressing them in hand-me-downs, sending them to inner-city schools, bringing them to peace demonstrations. None of the protests against nuclear weapons seemed to be having much effect. And so Philip Berrigan decided upon a new approach.

The first Plowshares action occurred on 9

September 1980, when the Berrigan brothers, Father Carl Kabat, Sister Anne Montgomery, and four others walked into a nuclear-warhead plant operated by General Electric in King of Prussia, Pennsylvania. The Berrigans had brought hammers, and when they found two missile nose cones designed to house nuclear warheads, they set out to fulfil the biblical injunction in Isaiah 2:4: 'And they shall beat their swords into plowshares, and their spears into pruning hooks: nation shall not lift up sword against nation, neither shall they learn war any more.' When security officers arrived, the activists stopped hammering the nose cones and didn't resist arrest. Philip Berrigan emptied a vial of his blood on some nearby blueprints.

The Plowshares Eight tried to use their trial to publicize the threat of nuclear weapons. But the crowds that had lined up to support the Berrigans during the Catonsville trial failed to materialize this time. Even the local religious community offered little help. Some of the defendants, housed at a Catholic women's college during the first week of the trial, were forced to leave by outraged alumnae. All eight were found guilty and sentenced to prison. Although the first Plowshares had been somewhat of a disappointment, a new template for direct action had been created – one that inspired more than a hundred similar assaults on the nation's nuclear enterprise.

Like American military operations, subsequent Plowshares actions were given names: 'Good News Plowshares', 'Prince of Peace Plowshares', 'Sacred Earth and Space Plowshares', 'Kairos Plowshares Two'. During 'Trident Nein', in July 1982, two nuns and seven accomplices broke into the General Dynamics Electric Boat shipyard, in Groton, Connecticut. Four of them paddled by canoe to a Trident submarine, climbed on the sub, hammered the missile hatches, poured blood on it, and rechristened it the USS *Auschwitz* with spray paint. Philip Berrigan encouraged Plowshares supporters to use their own blood as part of the ritual, often carried in baby bottles, 'to symbolize the death of innocent human beings'. The hammers had more than symbolic value; Berrigan hoped they'd do some real damage. In his view, weapons that could vaporize entire cities weren't 'legitimate property'.

At about four in the morning on Thanksgiving in 1983, Liz McAlister took part in her first Plowshares. She and six other protesters sneaked into Griffiss Air Force Base, in Rome, New York. It was remarkably easy: they didn't have to cut the barbed-wire fence; they just pulled the strands apart and climbed through. Someone who'd spent time at the base – where the Strategic Air Command kept B-52 bombers on alert with nuclear weapons – told McAlister where to go. The activists opened the unlocked door of a hangar and said, 'Hello, anybody home?' Nobody replied, so they walked in. They poured blood on the floor and on a B-52, pasted photographs of children on to the plane, hammered its bomb-bay doors, walked outside with an anti-nuclear banner, and awaited arrest. But nobody came to arrest them. After half an hour, one of them picked up a phone in the hangar, called the base switchboard, and wished the operator a 'Happy Thanksgiving'. Still nobody came. They wandered around outside for about an hour, singing songs and holding the banner, until security forces finally arrived.

McAlister spent more than two years in prison for her role in the Griffiss Plowshares. It was a difficult period for her children; the youngest was still a toddler. Berrigan supported his wife wholeheartedly. Both were willing to risk their lives for their faith, and he later argued that the break-in was motivated by love 'for all of the world's children'. Imprisoned six hours by car from Jonah House, McAlister wrote letters to her kids every day.

Other Plowshares followers received even harsher punishments for acts of non-violent resistance. On

12 November 1984, Father Carl Kabat broke into an unmanned, unguarded Minuteman II intercontinental-ballistic-missile complex forty miles east of Kansas City. He was accompanied by his older brother, Father Paul Kabat; Helen Woodson, a mother of eleven children; and Larry Cloud-Morgan, a Native American activist and spiritual leader of the Ojibwa tribe. As part of an action called 'Silo Pruning Hooks', they cut the lock off the perimeter fence with a bolt cutter, drove a yellow van trailing an air compressor onto the Minuteman site, and removed their tools. Carl Kabat attached a pneumatic drill to the air compressor and started chipping away pieces of the concrete silo door, while the others attacked equipment at the site with sledgehammers and wire cutters. The air compressor and the pneumatic drill died after half an hour. When two air-force security officers appeared, half an hour after that, they found the protesters kneeling on the silo door, singing, praying, and sharing bread. A banner draped over the fence said, 'Why do you do this evil thing?' The four Plowshares activists were convicted in federal court. Larry Cloud-Morgan was sentenced to eight years in prison, Father Paul Kabat to ten. Father Carl and Helen Woodson were given eighteen-year prison sentences.

Carl Kabat was released from prison after serving about seven years. He celebrated by breaking into the same Minuteman complex the following year, as part of an action called 'Good Friday Plowshares Missile Silo Witness'. He was sentenced to six months in a halfway house – and broke into a Minuteman complex outside Grand Forks, North Dakota, two years later, on April Fool's Day, wearing make-up, a wig, and a clown outfit. He was sentenced to prison for an additional five years. After gaining his freedom, having spent more than fifteen years in prison since his conviction as part of the original Plowshares Eight, Kabat proceeded to break into Minuteman complexes three more times, dressed as a clown. 'We are fools for Christ's sake,' he explained, quoting St Paul.

The American anti-nuclear movement reached its peak during the early 1980s, with large demonstrations nationwide and a rally in Central Park that attracted almost a million people. A nuclear war seemed not only possible but imminent, thanks to the Soviet Union's invasion of Afghanistan, the end of détente, and President Ronald Reagan's harsh rhetoric about the threat of 'an evil empire'. But Plowshares activists played a marginal role in the new movement, which relied on mainstream tactics, like circulating petitions and seeking new legislation, not direct action. The 'nuclear freeze' movement sought a halt to the arms race – not the abolition of nuclear weapons, the dismantling of a permanent war economy, world peace. Without much fanfare, Philip Berrigan kept getting arrested and going to prison. He still worked as a house painter to pay bills. The Jesus whom he worshipped was 'an outlaw', 'a non-violent revolutionary' who drove the money changers from the temple, challenged authority, and lived amid the poor. There was nothing meek or moderate about Him. Despite the end of the Cold War, the Plowshares actions continued, regardless of whether anyone noticed.

At the age of seventy-three, Philip Berrigan and five others broke into a Maine shipyard, pounded on the missile-hatch covers of a destroyer, and poured blood on it. They put photos of Hiroshima and Nagasaki victims on board the ship. Berrigan was convicted, imprisoned, released, and then imprisoned again after violating the terms of his parole. He spent most of 2001 behind bars for sneaking into a Maryland air base and applying a hammer to a fighter plane. The following year, at the age of seventy-nine, Berrigan passed away at Jonah House, after a short battle with cancer. 'I die with the conviction,' his final statement said, 'that nuclear weapons are the scourge of the earth; to mine for them, manufacture them, deploy them, use them, is a curse against God, the human family, and the Earth itself.'

## the burden of knowing

Once located in a Baltimore row house, Jonah House now sits a few miles away in the grounds of St Peter's Cemetery. The first burial at St Peters occurred in 1851, but the cemetery was abandoned in the late 1960s. It soon disappeared from view, as trees, bushes, vines, and poison ivy grew over the graves. The Baltimore Archdiocese allowed members of Jonah House to live there for free during the late 1990s. In return, they agreed to look after the cemetery. Most of its twenty-two acres have been cleared since then, at enormous effort, with some help from donkeys and goats. When I visited, in the spring of 2014, on a gorgeous, sunny day, the place felt bucolic – a well-tended stretch of green, surrounded by a tyre-recycling plant, a National Guard depot, and a low-income housing project. The two little homes occupied by Jonah House seemed peaceful and humble. Church services are held there every Sunday, the poor and the homeless are fed there every Tuesday, and the rest of the week is devoted to anti-war efforts, amid a landscape containing the remains of about 15,000 bodies.

At a table in the tidy kitchen of a house originally built for the cemetery caretaker, I had lunch with Liz McAlister, Sister Ardeth Platte, and Sister Carol Gilbert. Some of the food had been grown in their organic garden. All three women had short hair and wore the kind of clothes usually seen on Plowshares activists: sneakers, blue jeans, and T-shirts bearing a political slogan. Sister Ardeth's said 'NO WAR'. We talked about the history of the Plowshares movement, their involvement in direct action, the many places where they'd been jailed. Sister Carol, who's sixty-seven, and Sister Ardeth, who's seventy-eight, were both outraged and amused that their work on behalf of world peace had once landed them on a terrorist watch list. Their commitment to non-violence was complete. Although deeply upset by the attacks on Christian communities in Syria and Iraq, they thought that any violent response – even in self-defence, even to halt the slaughter of women and children – would be wrong. They both would rather die than have to kill. Like the other Plowshares activists I've encountered, there was nothing dour or severe about the two nuns and the former nun. They had an exuberant, often wry sense of humour. When asked how many times she'd been arrested, Liz McAlister, now seventy-five, replied, 'Not enough.'

Although the inclusion of Sister Ardeth and Sister Carol on a terrorist watch list was ridiculed in the press and later rescinded, the organizational skills of the Plowshares movement would be the envy of groups hoping to commit spectacular acts of terror on American soil. Plowshares actions aren't improvised or spontaneous; they're planned as much as a year in advance. The first step, according to one Plowshares veteran, involves 'wearing away of the ego, disarming the self, forming community, doing an in-depth analysis of our times'. The handful of volunteers pray together, read the Bible together, learn to trust one another without hesitation. They must be willing to risk their lives and sacrifice their freedom together. No one else can be harmed or endangered by the action – a fundamental rule. And everyone who plays a supporting role in it, often recruited from the more than 150 Catholic Worker houses nationwide, must be protected from arrest and conspiracy charges.

Once a strong bond has been forged among the group, a target is selected and then 'scoped' for months. While scoping it, Plowshares members will not only observe the security at a site but may test it, repeatedly. In preparation for one action, they secretly broke into an air-force base three times before publicly 'disarming' it with blood. Preparation for the trial is considered equally important. How the activists behave in court can establish the action's broader meaning, draw public attention to the cause, and put the government's behaviour on trial. The final step of a Plowshares action – prison – may be the most difficult and yet, in some ways, the most rewarding.

Sister Ardeth and Sister Carol have been arrested together more times than they can count, but they never seek to be incarcerated. They don't enjoy being in prison. An action that ends without time behind bars is called a 'freebie'. Instead of punishment or deterrence, however, they view prison as an opportunity. Tending the sick, the poor, and those in prison is the path to salvation, Jesus preached. Although prisons and jails are 'horrible places', Sister Carol told me, 'it's the closest as white, middle-class North Americans that we can really be with the poor'. They gain first-hand experience about life at the bottom of American society. They've been shackled and chained, strip-searched in front of male guards, locked in filthy cells with clogged toilets and vermin. They've listened helplessly to a dying friend, a fellow nun, cry for assistance from a nearby cell. The sisters look after the other inmates, trying to teach and empower them. But there have been lighter moments as well. Sister Carol got to know Martha Stewart behind bars. And Sister Ardeth practiced yoga with Piper Kerman, a convicted drug offender, who later wrote about her in *Orange Is the New Black*. 'Sister Ingalls', a character inspired by Sister Ardeth, appears in the television show based on the book.

While the behaviour of Plowshares activists may seem extreme, the rationale behind it is always the result of careful thought. Sister Ardeth spent most of her life working for change within the system before deciding to take more radical steps. Born and raised in central Michigan, she'd decided by the age of eleven that her life would be devoted to God and to serving others. She entered a convent after her freshman year of college, got a bachelor's degree and a master's, became a teacher, then a high-school principal in a poor, largely African-American and Latino neighbourhood of Saginaw, Michigan. Dorothy Day was her role model.

As a teacher and a principal in Saginaw, Sister Ardeth found herself in the middle of fistfights, gunfights, and race riots. She was elected to the city council, served on it for twelve years, helped found the city's first rape crisis centre and a shelter for battered women. She became mayor pro tem of Saginaw and enjoyed being a public servant, but her political career ended after Pope John Paul II decreed that members of the clergy could no longer run for elected office. Sister Ardeth helped to gain passage of a 1982 state law expressing Michigan's support for a nuclear freeze. The following year, nuclear weapons were deployed at Wurtsmith Air Force Base, in Michigan. She decided to oppose that move and joined forces with Sister Carol, whom she'd taught in high school. They were both Dominicans, members of a Catholic order whose motto is 'Veritas'. 'We preach truth to power,' Sister Ardeth likes to say.

Before long, the former city councilwoman and principal of a Catholic high school was dancing atop a nuclear-weapons bunker at Wurtsmith Air Force Base, singing, 'Jesus Christ has risen today!' Sister Ardeth and Sister Carol prayed at the gates of the base every day for three years. The fact that millions of people could be killed by nuclear weapons, at any moment, demanded that something radical be done. Sister Carol wanted somehow to pierce the widespread sense of denial, the wish to avoid 'the burden of knowing'.

At a Minuteman complex in eastern Colorado, Sister Ardeth, Sister Carol, and Sister Jackie Hudson

cut the lock off two fences, entered the site, and
drew crosses on the silo door with their blood.
Wearing white hazmat suits that said 'Disarmament
Specialist' on the front, they symbolically 'disarmed'
the site for forty-five minutes – hammering gently
to avoid causing any real damage – before being
arrested.

During the 'Gods of Metal Plowshares', Sister
Ardeth, Sister Carol, two priests, and a friend hurled
blood on to the bomb-bay doors of a B-52 at Andrews
Air Force Base, in Maryland. Although 'Gods of
Metal' could be the name of a Led Zeppelin cover
band, Sister Ardeth and Sister Carol chose it for a
serious purpose – to convey the idolatry of nuclear
weapons. Our reverence of their power, our blind
faith they will keep us safe, the sisters feared, may
lead to our annihilation.

After lunch, we walked along the dirt paths of
St Peter's. On the land that remains uncleared, top-
pled gravestones and cracked, ornate marble tombs
could be spotted amid the bushes and trees. Some
of the stones were so old and weathered that the
names of the dead could no longer be read. At
night, the place must feel like the setting of an
Edgar Allan Poe story. I asked the sisters if the lack
of publicity about Plowshares actions, the lack of
awareness about the nuclear threat, ever made

their work seem unsuccessful, their years in prison futile. Sister Carol acknowledged that the public apathy about nuclear weapons was frustrating. But she offered a different measure of success: are you truly living your faith?

I challenged the morality of breaking into high-security nuclear sites. What if someone got shot? What about the trauma a young security guard might experience, after realizing that he or she had killed a nun, not a terrorist? Sister Ardeth said that nobody had ever been harmed in the more than thirty years since the first Plowshares, and the Lord should be thanked for that. She betrayed no doubts. 'I will continue doing direct action for the rest of my life,' Sister Ardeth told me. 'If I can walk, you'll find me out there.'

The cleared section of St Peter's had a bright, cheery feel that day, more like a sculpture garden than a graveyard. A handful of people have been buried there since the cemetery reopened. The inscription on Philip Berrigan's gravestone gave his view of Christ's central message: 'Love one another.'

Before I left Jonah House, Sister Ardeth handed me a brown paper bag. I looked inside and saw an apple, an energy bar, and some nuts.

'It's a snack for your train ride to New York,' she said.

not far below my feet

A few weeks later, I drove through the missile fields of eastern Colorado and western Nebraska. Sister Ardeth and Sister Carol had urged me to go and see how lax the security still is at Minuteman launch complexes. The United States has 450 Minuteman III missiles at sites in Colorado, Nebraska, Wyoming, Montana, and North Dakota. The US Air Force's early intercontinental ballistic missiles – its Atlases, Titans, and Titan IIs – were overseen by launch crews that lived in underground control centres near the silos. When the Minuteman was being designed in the late 1950s, the air force decided the missiles should be remotely operated. The change would reduce the manpower necessary to operate them, enabling a single launch crew to command as many as fifty missiles. One of the new silos could be twelve miles away from its crew. The air force also chose to disperse Minuteman missiles widely throughout the Great Plains, so that a surprise attack by the Soviet Union couldn't easily destroy them all. In Montana, the new launch sites were built in an area extending for 14,000 square miles. Instead of being protected by armed guards, as in the Soviet Union, America's ballistic-missile complexes were unmanned, and built on one–acre plots of land, amid ranches and farms. Decisions made for reasons of efficiency and military strategy in the twentieth century couldn't anticipate the implications for nuclear terrorism in the twenty-first. Today, these missile sites are essentially unguarded nuclear-weapons-storage facilities. Some are within a quarter mile of private homes.

Using a map created by anti-nuclear activists in the late 1980s, I had little trouble finding Minuteman complexes. They are often visible from public roads. Soon I could spot one without the map – a cluster of poles in the middle of a field, surrounded by chain-link fence. What seemed extraordinary at first – a ballistic-missile complex right off the highway, in the middle of the prairie, just an hour or so east of Greeley, Colorado – soon became routine. At one Minuteman site, I parked my rental car, got out, and walked over to the nearby fence. The padlock on the gate could be cut open in seconds. Beyond it, the site's perimeter fence didn't look the slightest bit intimidating, despite a sign that said 'WARNING . . . Use of Deadly Force Authorized' in bright-red letters. Within a few minutes, you could remove a section of that fence big enough to drive a van, a digger, or a tractor-trailer onto the complex.

After 9/11, Remote Visual Assessment Cameras were installed at Minuteman complexes. While exploring the outskirts of the launch site, taking pictures, I kept expecting that someone would see me with those surveillance cameras and tell me in a loud, booming voice to stop. No one did.

It would be extremely difficult to break into a Minuteman launch facility and get anywhere near the missile – but not impossible. The complexes were designed to withstand the nearby detonation of a Soviet nuclear warhead. The silo door is a thick slab made from 110 tons of reinforced steel and concrete. A nearby Personnel Access Hatch leads to an underground entryway blocked by a 7-ton steel plug. You need one code to open the hatch, another to lower the plug out of the way. But the right explosives, properly employed, could eliminate the need for codes. A former member of a Minuteman security force told me that he could break into a complex, especially with help from an insider – a rogue launch officer, security officer, or mainten- ance technician. Once inside the silo, you would have to possess highly specialized skills and great ingenuity to launch a Minuteman missile or deton- ate its warhead. The missile would be easy to destroy, however, leaving behind a radioactive mess.

During the summer of 2013, a tactical-response force operating out of Malmstrom Air Force Base, in Montana, failed a major security test. According to a classified air-force report obtained by the Associated Press, the tactical force didn't respond 'effectively' to the simulated takeover of a Minuteman complex. The troops apparently couldn't recapture the silo from terrorists and didn't take 'all lawful actions necessary to immediately regain control of nuclear weapons'. The report criticized the training and leadership of the security force. Its commanding officer was removed from duty, and the entire strategic-missile wing at Malmstrom flunked its safety-and-security inspection. The air force now plans to deploy 300 additional airmen for nuclear-security tasks, responding to complaints that the current force is overworked, undermanned, and suffering from poor morale.

An air-force tactical-response force that's well trained and brilliantly led might still find it hard to cope with a terrorist attack on a Minuteman site – due to logistical problems and antiquated equipment. One of the missile complexes in Nebraska is about 125 miles from the air base in Wyoming where a tactical-response force is stationed. With luck, it would take about an hour or so for the force to reach that complex in an emergency. It could take a lot longer. And ideally, it wouldn't be raining heavily or the middle of the night. The UH-1N Huey helicopters that would carry the security force are, on average, forty-five years old. They are not properly equipped for night-time or bad-weather operations. They lack offensive weapons, defensive measures, modern avionics. They sometimes cannot fly the entire length of a missile field without being refuelled. Their crews rely on paper maps to navigate. And the Hueys are too small to carry a pilot, a co-pilot, a flight engineer, and a full tactical-response team.

Almost a decade ago, an air-force study concluded that the Hueys were responsible for 'missile field security vulnerabilities'. The same helicopters are also used to fly overhead and guard nuclear warheads being moved to and from missile sites. 'I cannot get security forces to the right places at the right time without a fast, capable, all-weather airlift capability,' the commander in charge of all the Minuteman complexes said, seven years ago. During the summer of 2014, the air force announced a plan to obtain used Blackhawk helicopters from the army for Minuteman security forces. But that plan remains unfunded, and the Vietnam-era Hueys may continue in service until 2020, if not longer.

For nearly forty minutes, I stood on the shoulder of a dirt road within throwing distance of a Minuteman complex. I didn't see another car on the road, let alone a security force with guns drawn. The short-grass prairie that stretched before me was windswept, gorgeous, dotted with small homes. You would never think that hidden beneath this rural American idyll, out of sight, out of mind, were scores of intercontinental ballistic missiles. Just yards away from my rental car, sitting not far below my feet, there was a thermonuclear warhead about twenty times more powerful than the bomb that destroyed Hiroshima, all set and ready to go. The only sound was the sound of the wind.

getting in trouble

Michael Walli worried about Sister Megan Rice.

The climb up Pine Ridge was steep, and Gregory Boertje-Obed led them through the dark woods without a map or a trail, guided only by flashlight.

Sister Megan was remarkably fit for an eighty-two-year-old, and she'd spent weeks training for this hike. But she had a mild heart condition. The two men had to stop every now and then so that she could catch her breath. When they resumed, Walli stayed behind her, keeping an eye on her, listening to her huff and puff. He was more fiery than most Plowshare activists, more intense, a believer in miracles and prophecy, a bold 'warrior for peace' like Philip Berrigan. Walli grew up on a farm in northern Michigan, the youngest of eight boys in his family. He also had six sisters. After dropping out of high school in 1967, at the age of eighteen, Walli enlisted in the army. Until then, his travels outside Michigan hadn't extended further than Wisconsin. Soon he was in Vietnam.

Two tours of duty left Walli alienated and disillusioned. He'd flown over jungles defoliated by Agent Orange, listened to B-52s carpet bombing at night, and witnessed firefights. After his return to the United States, Walli was in and out of veteran's hospitals for a while, suffering from post-traumatic stress disorder and a spiritual crisis. He took a series of jobs, working at a Christmas-card factory in Chicago, serving as a deckhand on merchant ships that plied the Great Lakes. In 1979, he began to help at a Chicago soup kitchen run by a Franciscan priest. It was a transformative experience. Walli joined the Third Order of St Francis, choosing to live in poverty and serve the poor. Eventually, he found his way to the Dorothy Day Catholic Worker House in

Washington DC, convinced that God had led him there. He stayed at various Catholic Worker houses along the East Coast and in the Midwest, gardening, doing manual labour, accumulating arrests for civil disobedience. He was strong and fit, with an intense look and a goatee. He helped clear the brush and cut down trees at St Peter's Cemetery.

Walli's first Plowshares action occurred in 2006, when he and Boertje-Obed broke into a Minuteman complex in North Dakota. They were dressed as clowns to honour Father Carl Kabat, who also wore a clown outfit, and joined them. They found the Personnel Access Hatch unlocked, opened it, hammered on an inner lock, and spray-painted messages on the silo door, such as 'God is not the author of confusion'. Walli got an eight-month sentence, Boertje-Obed twelve months, and Father Kabat fifteen.

A quarter of the way up Pine Ridge, Boertje-Obed saw a fence. It was chain link and not very intimidating, despite a 'No Trespassing' sign. The fence marked the boundary of the Y-12 complex. A winding dirt road ran beside it, patrolled by security forces. With a pair of red-handled bolt cutters, Boertje-Obed cut a vertical section of the fence along the fencepost, pushed open a gap, and helped the two others climb through it. Once they were all on Y-12 property, he neatly reattached the chain link to the fencepost with twine. That way, a security patrol driving past might not notice, in the darkness, that Y-12's security had been compromised.

Although Sister Megan had already been arrested between forty and fifty times, this was her first Plowshares action. And it was her idea. It had occurred to her about a year and a half earlier, while she was sitting in a Tacoma courtroom, watching the trial of five Plowshares activists who'd broken into Kitsap Naval Base. Located about thirty miles west of Seattle, Kitsap is the home port for more than half of America's Trident ballistic-missile submarines. During perhaps the worst nuclear-security lapse in the history of the US Navy, Father William 'Bix' Bichsel, Father Stephen Kelly, Sister Anne Montgomery, and two others had managed to sneak into the Strategic Weapons Facility Pacific – a storage area containing hundreds of nuclear warheads for Trident missiles. Those warheads don't have locking mechanisms. If a terrorist group detonated one at Kitsap, the blast not only would destroy the base and the Trident submarines but could also deposit lethal radioactive fallout on Seattle. If the group set off conventional explosives close to the warheads, a toxic cloud of plutonium might blanket the city. The Plowshares activists easily cut through

Kitsap's perimeter fence, hiked through the huge base for four hours, ignored warning signs outside the lethal force zone, cut through two more fences, and got to within about forty feet of the bunkers where the nuclear warheads are stored. Father Bix was eighty-one at the time. Sister Anne was eighty-three. Having survived two open-heart surgeries, Father Bix brought along his nitroglycerine tablets and paused to take some during the long hike. About twenty marines with automatic weapons stopped the activists, put hoods on them to prevent them from seeing any more of the top-secret facility, and made them lie on the ground for three and a half hours, while the base was searched for other intruders. When someone later said to Bix, 'Please, Father, don't get into any more trouble,' he laughed and replied, 'We're all in trouble.'

Listening to the testimony in court, Sister Megan thought not only that she could do that, she *had* to do it. Her activism had been limited mainly to protests at the US Army School of the Americas, in Georgia, and at the Nevada Test Site, where nuclear weapons were tested. She'd spent time in prison for civil disobedience. Born in 1930 and raised for the most part in Manhattan, a block away from Barnard College, Megan Rice had been taught from an early age to oppose racism, to care for the weak and the dispossessed. Her father was a professor of obstetrics at NYU, and he routinely treated indigent women at Bellevue Hospital. Her mother went to Barnard, earned a graduate degree at Columbia, and taught history at Hunter College. Rice's parents were friends with Dorothy Day before the launch of the *Catholic Worker*. They supported her work throughout the Great Depression and discussed social problems at her hospitality house every Friday night.

At the age of eighteen, Rice joined the Society of the Holy Child Jesus. She wanted to leave the comforts of Morningside Heights and teach at a girls' school in Africa. She earned a bachelor's degree at Fordham and a master's in biology at Boston College, then moved to Nigeria in 1962. Sister Megan helped to build the school where she later taught, slept in a classroom while it was under construction, and lived in a rural village without electricity or running water. She remained in Africa for most of the next thirty years. One of Sister Megan's uncles had spent time in Nagasaki, not long after its destruction by an atomic bomb, and his stories of the aftermath greatly disturbed her. When she moved back to the United States in the late 1980s, to help look after her mother, she got involved in protests at the Nevada Test Site – and persuaded her eighty-four-year-old mother to get arrested there, too. Sister Megan's time in Africa and the Nevada desert led her Catholic faith in a mystical, transcendental direction. She developed a profound love of nature, a belief in the interconnectedness of all things.

When Sister Megan raised the idea of a Plowshares action with Gregory Boertje-Obed, he agreed to join her. Boertje-Obed had already done five of them. His wife, Michele Naar-Obed, had done two, and they'd even done one together. They always tried to ensure that their daughter, Rachel, had at least one parent at home, not in prison. Sister Megan had lived at Jonah House for a while, helping to take care of Rachel. Michael Walli heard that Boertje-Obed and Sister Megan were going to do a Plowshares action and asked to join them. The three spent time together at spiritual retreats, prayed together, read the Bible together, enlisted more than half a dozen others for logistical support, and discussed potential targets. They considered a direct action at the Los Alamos National Laboratory, where nuclear weapons are designed, and at the Kansas City Plant, where weapon components are manufactured. But they chose the Y-12 complex to honour a late friend, Sister Jackie Hudson, who'd been arrested at the site the previous year – and to oppose plans to construct a vast uranium-processing plant there. The building would be used not only to disassemble and retire old weapons but also to refurbish them and, perhaps, build new weapons. The big, white, newly completed Highly Enriched Uranium Materials Facility seemed like a fine target for direct action. Sister Megan chose the name: 'Transform Now Plowshares'. She hoped it would begin the process of shutting down Y-12 and transforming the American empire from a source of bloodshed into one of world peace.

Boertje-Obed did the planning for the break-in. Using Google Earth and other satellite imagery, he looked for the best route to the uranium-storage facility. Two large white storage tanks on the northern edge of Y-12 promised to be a useful navigational aid. In addition to relying on the Internet, Boertje-Obed travelled to Oak Ridge and scoped the complex, taking notes on the security forces and their routines. He'd already broken into a missile complex and a naval air station, sneaked on to a submarine, and used a crowd of tourists as a diversion to get on to a battleship. The security at Y-12 was far more extensive than anything he'd ever confronted. Boertje-Obed wasn't sure if they could even get near the Protected Area.

More than an hour after leaving the church car park, the three activists reached the top of Pine Ridge.

Y-12 lay below them, lit with floodlights, bright as day. They could see the fences and barbed wire, the concrete barriers and guard towers. Boertje-Obed originally planned for them to walk down the hill and emerge from the woods a good distance from the towers. That approach, he thought, would be easier for Sister Megan. It would also minimize the risk of their getting shot. But Sister Megan seemed tired, and the fastest, most direct route now made more sense – straight down the hill. The uranium-storage facility was about a quarter of a mile away. They paused briefly and headed right towards it.

no rules at all

In the broad spectrum of nuclear terrorist acts, the takeover of a Minuteman III complex or the theft of a nuclear warhead from a Trident base isn't the most likely to occur. The detonation of a radiological dispersal device, a 'dirty bomb', would be one of the easiest to pull off. All you need are some conventional explosives and a small amount of a radioactive material. About half a dozen radio-isotopes routinely used for medical, scientific, and commercial purposes – including a radioactive element found in household smoke detectors – could be utilized to make a dirty bomb. But the easiest forms of terrorism are also the least conse-quential. The conventional explosives in a dirty bomb would pose the greatest immediate risk to anyone near the detonation. Even in a densely populated city, the radioactive dust produced by a dirty bomb would cause serious, long-term harm to perhaps a few hundred people. Cleaning up after such a bomb, however, could cost billions of dol-lars. It would provoke a great deal of anxiety. And real estate in the contaminated area would lose much of its value.

Terrorists seeking to cause a radiological disaster, like the one at Fukushima or Chernobyl, would find it much harder to accomplish than making a dirty bomb. They might have to hack the control systems at a nuclear power plant, use explosives to rupture the plant's containment vessel, or drain the water from a pool storing its spent fuel rods. Without the water, the fuel rods could spontaneously ignite, releasing as much as five times the amount of harmful radioactivity contained in the reactor's core.

The detonation of a nuclear weapon would be the most difficult type of nuclear terrorism to achieve. It would also be the most lethal and dramatic. But stealing a weapon from a military base would be a real challenge. Even if you somehow obtained the weapon, you'd have to figure out how to detonate it. You'd need help from someone who knew a thing or two about nuclear weapons. Creating an 'improvised nuclear device', a homemade atomic bomb, presents its own set of challenges. Only a couple of fissile materials can readily be used to generate the extraordinary destructive force of a nuclear weapon. Those materials are not widely found in nature. Plutonium-239 is produced in a nuclear reactor, and a thousand pounds of natural uranium contain just seven pounds of uranium-235, the isotope used in nuclear weapons. Although the physicists at Los Alamos gained acclaim for design-ing the first atomic bombs, the chemists and engineers at Oak Ridge and at the Hanford Site, in Washington – who figured out how to produce fissile material – made those weapons possible. Seventy years later, hundreds of millions of dollars and great technical ability are still necessary to make plutonium-239 or to enrich uranium until it reaches weapons grade (about 90 per cent uranium-235). Instead of dealing with all that hassle and expense, terrorists would be far more likely to steal fissile materials or buy them on the black market.

Plutonium is more efficient than uranium at creating a nuclear explosion. But plutonium is far more toxic, dangerous to handle, difficult to fabricate. And nuclear-weapon designs that use plutonium tend to be more complex. Little Boy, the uranium weapon used to destroy Hiroshima, had a design so simple that it didn't need to be fully tested before it was dropped. Acquiring the weapons-grade uranium was the hard part; detonating it was relatively easy. Luis Alvarez, a Nobel Prize-winning physicist who played a crucial role in the Manhattan Project, later warned that if terrorists obtained weapons-grade uranium, they wouldn't need to be experts in nuclear-weapon design. In fact, Alvarez wrote, they'd have 'a good chance of setting off a high-yield explosion simply by dropping one half of the material on to the other half'. Terrorists hoping to survive the nuclear blast would have to design and build a complicated machine – a weapon that could be safely transported, armed near the target, and remotely detonated from miles away. Those willing to be vaporized and die for the cause would have fewer technical worries.

The threat of nuclear terrorism has been a

concern since the early days of the atomic era. During a closed Senate hearing in 1946, J. Robert Oppenheimer, the scientific director of the Manhattan Project, was asked whether three or four people could smuggle into New York City the parts necessary to build a nuclear weapon. 'Of course it could be done,' he said, and it would be almost impossible to prevent. 'The only instrument that would enable an inspector to find out if a packing crate contained an atomic bomb is a screwdriver.' The hunt for terrorists or blackmailers who've got a nuclear weapon became a familiar plot element in pulp novels like *The Smuggled Atom Bomb* (1948), *One of Our H-Bombs Is Missing* (1955), and *The Day They H-Bombed Los Angeles* (1961). But scenarios that seemed to belong in B-movies or pulp fiction were taken seriously by the National Security Council (NSC). In a top-secret document, the NSC recommended in 1953 that efforts 'to develop an active technical device for the detection of fissionable material should proceed with the utmost urgency'. The Soviet Union, it was feared, might try to smuggle a nuclear weapon into the United States or secretly build one here and then detonate it. A classified report prepared for the air force later warned that the Soviets might sabotage an American nuclear weapon, hoping to inspire terror, diminish public support for American foreign policy, and 'increase public pressures . . . for nuclear disarmament'.

For most of the Cold War, however, nuclear threats from outside the United States seemed more pressing than those that might emerge within it. According to Matthew Bunn, a nuclear-security expert and a professor at Harvard University's John F. Kennedy School of Government, during the 1950s and 1960s, 'the Atomic Energy Commission (AEC) literally imposed *no rules at all* concerning how private companies with weapons-usable nuclear material had to secure such stocks'. The AEC assumed that the financial value of the fissile material would encourage companies to safeguard it carefully. While researching 'The Curve of Binding Energy' for the *New Yorker* magazine in 1972, John McPhee found that plutonium was being shipped across the United States without armed guards – and that two people with guns and a pickup truck could steal as much plutonium as their truck could carry. The terrorist attack on the Munich Olympics that year and the subsequent publication of McPhee's work prompted much tougher federal oversight of fissile materials. The rise of terrorism in the following decades and the 9/11 attacks tightened the security even further.

And yet until the opening of the Highly Enriched Uranium Materials Facility in 2010, tons of weapons-grade uranium were still being stored at Y-12 in a wooden building constructed during the Manhattan Project.

The traditional reliance on 'guns, gates, and guards' for nuclear security may overlook a serious vulnerability at nuclear sites: the insider threat. Scott D. Sagan, a nuclear-weapons expert and a professor of political science at Stanford University, thinks that the security culture at a facility is as important as its security equipment. Those who work at a nuclear site are the most familiar with its security weaknesses. Managers too often become complacent about long-time employees and don't consider the possibility that someone may be black-mailed or coerced into helping terrorists. As one security expert notes: 'Any vulnerability assessment which finds no vulnerabilities or only a few is worthless and wrong.'

The designs of the first atomic bombs were stolen by insiders at Los Alamos and shared with the Soviet Union. Insiders at Oak Ridge provided the Soviets with the details of how to make weapons-grade uranium. More recently, Edward Snowden, a private contractor working for the National Security Agency, gained access to some of its most highly classified secrets. The NSA is responsible not only for generating the launch codes for America's nuclear weapons but also for designing the equipment that decrypts the codes. In 2013, two high-level nuclear commanders were removed from duty for behaviour that could have exposed them to blackmail: illegal gambling in one case, excessive alcohol consumption with young Russian women in the other. A group of hackers known as 'Team Digi7al' and 'Team Havok' managed to hack websites belonging to the US Navy, the Los Alamos National Laboratory, the United States National Geospatial-Intelligence Agency, the Department of Homeland Security, and the Library of Congress. One of the group's members turned out to be Nicholas Knight, a sailor deployed on the USS *Harry S Truman*. Knight was a systems administrator for the computers running the aircraft carrier's nuclear reactor.

During the 1960s, when the Atomic Energy Commission trusted that private companies would effectively secure their own fissile material, hundreds of pounds of weapons-grade uranium went missing from the Nuclear Materials and Equipment Corporation plant in Apollo, Pennsylvania. There is strong evidence that the uranium was shipped to Israel, with help from insiders at the plant.

According to the *Bulletin of the Atomic Scientists*, President Gerald Ford discussed the theft with James Connor, an aide who'd been an official at the AEC. 'The good news is that Israel definitely has the Bomb and can take care of itself,' Connor told the president. 'The bad news is that the stuff came from Pennsylvania.'

for peace not war

The Y-12 complex had layered security. The closer you got to the Protected Area, the more intense the security became. The barriers, fences, cameras, and motion detectors weren't designed to prevent an intrusion. They were supposed to delay it, reveal it, and draw the necessary security forces to stop it.

The woods ended at the bottom of the hill. Once the three Plowshares activists emerged from the shadow of the last trees, they'd have to walk into a flat, clear, brightly lit area, cross Bear Creek Road, and cut through three more fences to reach the Protected Area. The uranium-storage facility loomed ahead, the great white castle, with guards bearing automatic weapons in its towers.

The three hid in tall grass as patrol cars passed. And then Boertje-Obed led the others across the road, over a low concrete barrier, to a chain-link fence, roughly eight feet high. It was the first line of the high-tech Perimeter Intrusion Detection and Assessment System. As Boertje-Obed began to cut the fence, he expected sirens and alarms to go off. But none did, and while he continued to cut the fence, Walli draped a banner on it. The banner had a drawing of a nuclear weapon and the words 'Never again'.

The next fence looked more formidable. A thick cable was interlaced with chain link. Beyond the fence was a gravel area, a clear zone, and then another fence.

Boertje-Obed had a moment of doubt. He wondered if this second fence was electrified. Maybe they should turn around and head back to the ridge, he thought. We're not going to be able to cut through this one without being detected.

Walli and Sister Megan had quietly followed Boertje-Obed, assuming he knew what to do and where to go.

'Well, it's worth a try,' Boertje-Obed told himself.

The bolt cutters snipped the fence, and no klaxons sounded.

Sister Megan had felt all along that they were being guided by the Holy Spirit.

As Boertje-Obed cut through the last fence, he was feeling focused and amazed. It was bright as daylight, and yet nobody had spotted them. The uranium-storage facility was about forty feet away, across a stretch of flat, wide-open asphalt. They were almost there.

The walls of the building were soon being decorated with spray paint and blood. It was Tom Lewis's blood, drawn from his arm four years earlier, not long before he died. Lewis had been one of the Catonsville Nine, an artist, and a Plowshares activist arrested numerous times. From his deathbed, Lewis had asked that his blood be used in one last direct action. The blood was frozen, saved, thawed, and poured into six baby bottles carried in backpacks to Y-12. Now it dripped down the white walls.

'WORK FOR PEACE NOT WAR' was spray painted onto the building in large black letters, along with 'PLOWSHARES PLEASE ISAIAH' and 'THE FRUIT OF JUSTICE IS PEACE'. In red letters, 'WOE TO THE EMPIRE OF BLOOD' was scrawled across another wall.

Boertje-Obed removed a small sledgehammer from his pocket and struck a corner of the building. Nothing happened. He tried again, hit it about a dozen times, and knocked off a piece of concrete about a foot long. The others hammered the building lightly, and Sister Megan helped to drape crime-scene tape across it. They placed Bibles and white roses on the ground to commemorate the White Rose, a German student group that had opposed Hitler and promoted non-violent resistance. They did all this for about ten minutes, waiting for someone to show up.

A patrol car appeared, at about five in the morning, and they began to sing, 'This little light of mine, let it shine all around Y-12.'

the older one, with the goatee

A security officer, Kirk Garland, had been asked to check the fences near the north side of the uranium-storage building, where an alarm had been triggered. When he got there, three people approached his SUV, and Garland saw the slogans sprayed on the walls. He'd worked at federal nuclear facilities for almost thirty years and immediately assumed these people were protesters, not members of Al Qaeda. As he sat in the parked SUV, his supervisor called, and Garland asked for backup. The three stood beside his car door, said they'd been sent by God, offered him some bread, and read a statement.

'Today, through our non-violent action, we,

Transform Now Plowshares, indict the US Government nuclear-modernization program,' it began.

Garland told them not to make any sudden move-
ments or remove anything from their backpacks. But
the situation became chaotic. After the statement
was finished, someone started reading passages from
the Bible to him. The elderly woman told Garland
she had a heart condition. One of the men ignored
his instructions, pulled candles out of a backpack, lit
them, and offered him one.

Sergeant Chad Riggs was sitting in his office
when a supervisor called and said something was
going on at the uranium-storage facility. Garland
needed backup. As Riggs drove his Chevy Tahoe
around the corner of the building, he saw Garland's
vehicle, three people standing near it, the spray
paint and blood on the walls.

Riggs jumped out of the Tahoe, drew his sidearm,
ordered the three suspects to lie on the ground, and
demanded to see their hands. At the same time, he
got on the radio and called for additional officers.
Once the suspects were on the ground, he told
them to crawl away from the backpacks and gear.
'There appear to be intruders in the Protected Area,'
he said over the radio.

Concerned that a sniper might be hiding somewhere up in the hills, Sergeant Riggs asked Garland

to provide cover. Riggs quickly put on his body armour and retrieved his M4 assault rifle from the Tahoe. Then he ordered Garland to put on body armour, too.

Riggs had a gut feeling that one of the men, the older one, with the goatee, might be dangerous. He ordered Garland to take the man off to the side and handcuff him.

When backup units arrived, the other man and the elderly woman were cuffed. For the next five hours, the suspects sat on the ground or stood briefly, hands secured behind their backs. At about ten in the morning, they were provided with plastic chairs.

justified

After spending the weekend in the Blount County Jail, Walli, Boertje-Obed, and Sister Megan were brought to federal court in shackles. They were charged with trespassing on government property, a misdemeanour. More serious charges were likely to be filed soon. Assistant US Attorney Melissa Kirby asked the judge not to release them from jail. They were repeat offenders. They lived in other parts of the country, presented a flight risk, and could pose a 'danger to the community'.

A few days later, Judge C. Clifford Shirley ignored the prosecutor's objections and ruled that the defendants should be released once they entered a plea. Sister Megan and Walli pleaded not guilty.

'I plead justified because the building of nuclear weapons is a war crime,' Boertje-Obed said in court. 'I plead for the downtrodden around the world who suffer the consequences of our nuclear weapons.'

The judge entered a plea of not guilty for him.

Walli and Sister Megan later walked free. Boertje-Obed chose to remain in jail.


tolerating the intolerable


Within days, the Plowshares action at Y-12 attracted international attention. The fact that an eighty-two-year-old nun had broken into a high-security nuclear-weapons complex seemed unbelievable. But to some people familiar with the security arrangements at Y-12 the intrusion was the logical result of mismanagement that had plagued the facility for years. Although the federal government owned the land, most of the buildings, the equipment, and the fissile material at the Y-12 complex, private contractors now ran the facility for profit. During the Cold War, the weapons laboratories had been managed through an unusual combination of public and private oversight. The Los Alamos Scientific Laboratory, for example, was operated by the University of California. Sandia Laboratory was run by subsidiaries of AT&T at no charge to the government. The weapons labs and manufacturing plants were run like non-profits: they were supposed to serve the national interest. A decade ago, the management of America's nuclear enterprise was largely privatized – a change that was spurred by promises of greater efficiency. A new federal agency, the National Nuclear Security Administration, was created to oversee the private contractors. And the management of nuclear-security forces was increasingly privatized as well.

During the summer of 2012, when the break-in occurred at Y-12, Wackenhut Services Inc. was responsible for the security officers at the site. The company had been founded in the early 1950s by George Wackenhut, a former FBI agent who pioneered the private security industry, gaining contracts from corporations and federal agencies, establishing close ties with the FBI and the CIA. But in 2012, Wackenhut Services was no longer an American company. It had been acquired by Group 4 Falck, once a Danish company, now a British one, known as G4S. In addition to protecting the

weapons-grade uranium at Y-12 through a subsid-
iary, G4S provided security at rock concerts and
banks and shopping malls, operated private prisons,
employed armed guards to defend embassies in
Afghanistan and Iraq. The company operated in
more than 125 countries. Through mergers and
acquisitions, it had rapidly become the third-largest
private employer in the world, after Walmart and
Foxconn. Most people had never heard of G4S until
a few weeks before the Y-12 intrusion, when the
company mishandled the security arrangements
for the London Olympic Games. G4S trainees were
allegedly caught cheating on bomb-detection tests,
a charge that the company later denied. G4S failed
to hire the number of security guards it had promised, and the British military had to send 3,500
troops to the Olympics at the last minute.

Wackenhut's performance at Y-12 was not much
better. A 2004 report by the Department of Energy's
Office of Inspector General found that security officers at Y-12 had been cheating on performance tests
for years. Before responding to mock attacks, Wackenhut officers were told in advance which building
at Y-12 would be targeted, which wall of the building would be attacked, and whether their adversaries
would use diversionary tactics. In at least one case,
the information allowed officers to prepare an

effective response weeks in advance. And before the tests, members of the security force allegedly disabled their Multiple Integrated Laser Engagement System gear – removing the batteries, inserting the batteries backwards, covering the laser sensors with tape or Vaseline – so that during a simulated gunfight they could not be 'shot'. Failing a performance test might reduce Wackenhut's fee from the government. Wackenhut employees not only cheated on the tests, they came up with the tests. But the company disputed the findings of the Inspector General's report.

On the night of the Y-12 break-in, a camera that would have enabled security personnel to spot the intruders was out of commission. According to a document obtained by Frank Munger, a reporter at the Knoxville *News Sentinel*, about a fifth of the cameras on the fences surrounding the Protected Area were not working that night. One camera did capture someone climbing through a fence. But the security officer who might have seen the image was talking to another officer, not looking at his screen. Cameras and motion detectors at the site had been broken for months. The security equipment was maintained by Babcock & Wilcox, a private contractor that managed Y-12, while the officers who relied on the equipment worked for Wackenhut.

Poor communication between the two firms con-
tributed to long delays whenever something needed
to be fixed. And it wasn't always clear who was
responsible for getting it fixed. The Plowshares
activists did set off a number of alarms. But security
officers ignored them, because hundreds of false
alarms occurred at Y-12 every month. Officers stationed inside the uranium-storage facility heard the
hammering on the wall. But they assumed that the
sounds were being made by workmen doing
maintenance.

Just a few months before the break-in, the
National Nuclear Security Administration had given
Wackenhut high scores in a review of its security
performance at Y-12, granting the company a large
fee. Wackenhut was planning to eliminate the jobs
of seventy guards at Y-12, in order to cut costs. Not
long after the break-in, an investigation by the
Department of Energy's Office of Inspector General
found that, once again, Wackenhut security guards
at Y-12 had been caught cheating on their performance tests. According to a follow-up report by the
Inspector General, the guards later testified that
they had 'no intent to cheat'.

Asked by the Secretary of Energy to evaluate the
multiple security failures at Y-12, Norman R. Augustine, a former under-secretary of the army and

former chief executive of Lockheed Martin, concluded that the root of the problem was clear: 'a pervasive culture of tolerating the intolerable and accepting the unacceptable'. Of all the failure analyses that Augustine had conducted in his long career, 'none had been more difficult for me to comprehend than this one'. He considered himself a strong defender of the free-enterprise system but thought that the protection of nuclear weapons and fissile materials was so important that it should be handled by the federal government, not by private contractors.

sabotage!

During the second week of September 2012, congressional hearings were held to discuss the security at Y-12. Representative Michael Turner, a Republican from Ohio, opened one of the hearings by saying, 'It is outrageous to think that the greatest threat to the American public from weapons of mass destruction may be the incompetence of DOE security . . . This must not happen again.' Sister Megan Rice and Michael Walli attended the hearings but weren't asked to testify. Nevertheless, Representative Joe Barton, a Republican from Texas, acknowledged that Sister Megan was in the audience. 'Would you please stand up, ma'am?' he asked. 'We want to thank you for pointing out some of the problems in our security.' Representative Edward Markey, a Democrat from Massachusetts, was even more effusive. Addressing Sister Megan directly, Markey said, 'Thank you for your actions. Thank you for your willingness to focus attention on this nuclear-weapons build-up . . . We thank you for your courage . . . you should be praised because that's ultimately what the Sermon on the Mount is all about.'

Gregory Boertje-Obed finally sought to get out of jail that week. He wanted to see his family and start preparing a defense. He promised the judge that he wouldn't break into Y-12 again or commit other acts of civil disobedience while awaiting trial. Assistant US Attorney Melissa Kirby opposed the release, claiming that such promises were 'disingenuous'. Persuaded that Boertje-Obed would keep his word, the judge let him go see his family.

A federal grand jury had already handed down further indictments. In addition to the misdemeanour trespassing charge, the protesters now faced two felony counts. The first was for 'wilfully and maliciously' destroying property at Y-12. The second was for committing a 'depredation against property of the United States and of the United States Department of Energy, National Nuclear Security Administration, Y-12 National Security Complex . . . in an amount exceeding $1,000'. To 'depredate' means 'to lay waste: plunder, ravage,' according to *Webster's* dictionary. The felony counts could lead to a prison sentence of fifteen years. And as lawyers representing the activists discussed a possible plea bargain with the US Attorney's Office in Knoxville, the government threatened to file an even more serious charge: sabotage.

Although the Sabotage Act was passed in 1918, at the height of the First World War, when America was gripped with the fear of German spies, the law has rarely been used against people who've actually committed sabotage. Instead, it has been used against labour organizers, opponents of the Vietnam War, and anti-nuclear activists. The statute's broad definition of sabotage – attempting or committing an act with the 'intent to injure, interfere with, or obstruct the national defence of the United States' – has made the law a useful tool for punishing acts of civil disobedience.

Walli, Boertje-Obed, and Sister Megan refused to accept a plea bargain. They wanted a trial by jury. The government quickly dropped the trespassing charge and added sabotage to the indictment.

William P. Quigley, the attorney representing Walli, asked the judge to throw out the sabotage charge. A professor of law at Loyola University New Orleans, Quigley argued that the sabotage law was being selectively applied in this case. Plowshares activists who had committed similar non-violent acts generally weren't accused of sabotage. Father Bix had been given a three-month prison sentence after breaking into the nuclear-weapons storage area at Kitsap in 2009. Sister Megan and the others now faced a possible thirty-five years behind bars.

Quigley was an expert on the 'necessity defence' and hoped to use it in the Y-12 case. Dating back centuries to English common law, the defence enabled someone to be found innocent if a crime had been committed to avoid a greater harm. Crimes of necessity might include tossing valuable cargo overboard to prevent a ship from sinking, breaking into a pharmacy to obtain life-saving medicine for someone in an emergency, shattering a shop window to escape a fire. Sir Walter Scott, who was a judge as well as a novelist, believed that 'necessity creates the law, it supersedes rules; and whatever is *reasonable* and *just* in such cases, is likewise *legal*'.

The three activists had broken into Y-12, Quigley planned to argue, in order to avoid a nuclear holocaust. He had defended peace activists since the early 1980s and sympathized with many of their views. The necessity defence was occasionally successful in state courts. Protesters had been found not guilty after blocking access to a cruise-missile plant in Michigan, handing out leaflets at a nuclear-weapons plant in Massachusetts, and trespassing at a Salt Lake City factory that made rocket engines for Trident missiles. In each of those cases, a jury heard the defendant's moral, political, and religious reasons for taking action and voted to acquit.

When two Plowshares activists snuck into a Sperry Corporation plant in Minnesota and destroyed a computer built for a Trident submarine, they were allowed to mount a necessity defence in federal court – and they were found guilty by the jury. The judge, Miles Lord, was more open to their arguments. He refused to accept 'that there is something sacred about a bomb and that those who raise their voices or their hands against it should be struck down as enemies of the people'. Judge Lord had overseen a case a few months earlier in which Sperry was accused of embezzling $3.6 million from the federal government, and yet none of the company's executives were punished. The two Plowshares activists walked free with six months of unsupervised parole.

Since the early 1990s, however, federal judges have rarely permitted claims of necessity to be used in civil-disobedience cases. The United States Court of Appeals for the Ninth Circuit has imposed a standard of proving necessity that's almost impossible to meet. Before being allowed to bring a necessity defence before a jury, the defendant must persuade a judge that the harm to be avoided was imminent, that the illegal act would actually prevent the greater harm, and that there were no legal alternatives to breaking the law. The tough standard of proof has limited the influence of juries in civil-disobedience cases and empowered federal judges. It has also reduced the possibility that defendants will be found not guilty.

At a pre-trial hearing, Boertje-Obed, representing himself, asked the court to permit the use of the necessity defence. The government had already submitted a brief seeking to preclude that defence. It would keep the jury from hearing evidence about the morality of nuclear weapons, international law or the defendants' political and religious beliefs. The preparation for war crimes is a crime, Boertje-Obed argued, citing one of the Nuremberg principles used to prosecute the leadership of Nazi Germany. 'So, when you build a nuclear weapon, you are planning and preparing to commit mass murder,' he said. 'You are giving your assent to the killing of civilians.'

In response to those arguments, Assistant US Attorney Jeffrey E. Theodore, citing Justice John Paul Stevens, portrayed all civil disobedience as anti-democratic. It was 'a form of arrogance which organized society cannot tolerate'. Theodore suggested that allowing the necessity defence in this case might justify its use by activists who had blown up an abortion clinic. 'These [Plowshares] defendants, they know,' he told the court. 'They're all recidivists when it comes to this . . . They want to present their anti-nuclear agenda and they want the biggest forum they can get in order to do that. And the more they can espouse their views about the operations at Y-12, or the horrors of nuclear weapons and things like that . . . the happier they are.'

Judge Shirley forbade the use of the necessity defence and let the sabotage charge stand.

Walli, Boertje-Obed, and Sister Megan didn't deny breaking into Y-12, cutting the fences, and spraying graffiti. At their trial, in May 2013, they described those actions matter-of-factly. The charge of damaging government property would be hard to beat. To obtain a guilty verdict on the other two charges, the government had to prove that repairing the damage at Y-12 cost more than a thousand dollars and that the three activists wilfully set out to harm the national defence of the United States.

Before the trial, the government had claimed that the damage at Y-12 had cost an estimated $70,000 to repair. During the trial, Assistant US Attorney Kirby said, 'It was probably closer to the ballpark of $8,000 worth of damage.' According to subsequent testimony, more than $7,000 of that amount was labour costs, and the labour was performed by Y-12 employees. The cost of the materials purchased to mend the broken fences and scrub the white walls clean was less impressive. It came to about $760.

As for the sabotage charge, Kirby asserted that harming the national defence of the United States had been the central aim of the protesters: 'their whole purpose was to interfere with or obstruct Y-12 operations'. The facility had to be shut down for two weeks after the intrusion; a delivery of special nuclear materials had been delayed; the reputation of Y-12, the National Nuclear Security Administration, and the United States had been hurt. The defence attorneys countered that all those consequences were impossible to foresee, since the three protesters were surprised they could even get into the facility, let alone disrupt it. Far from endangering the country, the break-in had improved the security at Y-12. And if calling for the abolition of nuclear weapons threatened the national defence of the United States, then people like Henry Kissinger were saboteurs, too.

The trial was notable mostly for what it revealed about the participants. Boertje-Obed asked the jury to consider the philosophical difference between 'real security' and 'false security'. Walli called his service in Vietnam 'employment as a terrorist for the United States Government'. He compared the morality of cutting the fences at Y-12 to that of cutting fences at Auschwitz. When asked by Assistant US Attorney Theodore whether he had protested at nuclear-weapons facilities in other countries, Walli said that he had not, adding, 'I'm an indigent person . . . It's pretty pricey going to Russia or North Korea.' Theodore later compared the break-in at Y-12 to the attacks on 9/11. Since both had led to tighter security, he asked the jury: 'Does that mean 9/11 was a good thing?'

From the witness stand, Sister Megan described her mystical, nature-loving form of Catholicism. All living things are miraculous and interconnected, she believed. 'I was aware of every moment being an imminent threat to the life and harmony of the planet,' Sister Megan said under cross-examination, explaining why she broke into

Y-12. 'Every moment, as we sit here now, is an imminent threat to the life of the planet, which is sacred.'

A few moments earlier, Kirby had asked, 'What do you think about what they do at Y-12?'

'I think with sadness that they are making a huge amount of money,' Sister Megan said.

Walli, Boertje-Obed, and Sister Megan were convicted by the jury on all counts.

Because of the conviction for attacking government property, the three were now classified as violent offenders and couldn't be at liberty while the verdict was appealed. They were handcuffed, shackled, and led from the courtroom to jail.


no way to guarantee


On 6 September 2014, members of Al Qaeda in the Indian subcontinent tried to hijack two warships belonging to the Pakistan Navy. The terrorists planned to use one of the frigates, the PNS *Zulfiqar*, to attack American naval vessels with its guided missiles and 72 mm guns; the other frigate, the PNS *Aslat*, would attack Indian ships. According to the Government of Pakistan, the plot was foiled while the *Zulfiqar* was still moored at a Karachi naval base.

An Al Qaeda press release told a different story, claiming the failed hijackings occurred while the frigates were at sea. Both accounts agreed that the terrorist act ended with a fierce gun battle – and that members of Al Qaeda had infiltrated the Pakistan Navy. One of the ringleaders was a lieutenant, and more than a dozen other officers and sailors may have been involved in the scheme. In 2011, members of another terrorist group, Tehrik-i-Taliban, attacked a naval air base in Karachi to avenge the death of Osama bin Laden, destroying aircraft and eluding authorities for seventeen hours. The terrorists had most likely been helped by insiders at the base. In October 2009, ten militants entered the central headquarters of the Pakistan Army in broad daylight, wearing military uniforms and carrying fake IDs. They took dozens of hostages, killed high-ranking officers, and maintained control of a building there for eighteen hours. The two leading commanders of Pakistan's nuclear forces were stationed at the base.

The United States is far more open and transparent about its nuclear-weapons programmes than any other nation, enabling discussion and debate about the security at its nuclear sites. But that openness, and the many security problems it has revealed, should not imply that the greatest threat of nuclear terrorism comes from sites in the United States. On the contrary, America may have the best nuclear-security systems in the world. The management challenges that the United States has faced are now being encountered by every other country that possesses nuclear weapons.

Pakistan tops the list of nations that cause terrorism experts the greatest concern. It has the world's fastest-growing nuclear arsenal. It has dispersed nuclear weapons to multiple locations, making them less vulnerable to destruction by a foreign nation but more vulnerable to theft by terrorists. It has extremist groups seeking to infiltrate the military. And few people outside Pakistan know how its nuclear enterprise is really being run. One of the top-secret documents obtained by Edward Snowden in 2013 says that American intelligence agencies have little 'knowledge of the security of Pakistan's nuclear weapons and associated material'. The question deeply concerns Russia as well. A classified State Department document released by WikiLeaks describes a meeting between Russian and American diplomats in Washington. 'Islamists are not only seeking power in Pakistan but are also trying to get their hands on nuclear materials,' an official at Russia's Ministry of Foreign Affairs said. Perhaps 125,000 people were directly involved in Pakistan's nuclear-weapons and missile programmes. The Russian official warned that 'regardless of the clearance process for these people, there is no way to guarantee that all are 100% loyal'.

Remarkably little is known about the security arrangements at India's nuclear facilities. Its weapons aren't as widely dispersed as Pakistan's. But in both countries terrorists and extremists are more likely to seek plutonium and weapons-grade uranium. Fissile materials are easier to steal than nuclear weapons and much lighter to carry. An improvised explosive device can be made with just 120 pounds of uranium or 20 pounds of plutonium. And those amounts don't have to be stolen all at once. An insider at a nuclear facility could secretly remove a few ounces of fissile material every so often and accumulate a significant amount of it over time.

India and Pakistan aren't the only nuclear-weapons states that pose major security risks. One of the United Kingdom's most important nuclear facilities is reached by a single, narrow country road – and if that road's blocked, the security forces at the site could have a long wait for reinforcements during a terrorist attack. In 2013, *Le Télégramme*, a newspaper in Brittany, exposed a litany of security problems at Île Longue, France's ballistic-missile-submarine base. Journalists at the paper managed to create a phony access badge and gain access to the top-secret base. They discovered that trucks entering the site were rarely checked; that inexperienced, poorly paid, volunteer deputy policemen were guarding the site; that some of the guards had only fifteen days of training; that radiation alarms routinely went off and were ignored; and that the site lacked weaponry that could protect the submarines from an aerial attack. During a security test the previous year, French commandos had managed to get into the base, place an explosive device on a submarine carrying nuclear warheads, and leave without being detected.

In 2010, at a NATO air base in Belgium, peace activists climbed over one fence, cut through a second, and entered a hardened shelter containing nuclear-weapon vaults. The 'Bomspotters' put anti-nuclear stickers on the shelter walls. They spent an hour wandering the air base before being stopped, and posted a video of their intrusion on YouTube. The video revealed that the soldier who stopped them was carrying an unloaded rifle. The security of NATO nuclear weapons has caused concern for decades. The weapon vaults can be breached with high explosives, if you have enough time and knowhow. And terrorists aren't the only threat: America's NATO allies have been suspected, on at least one occasion, of seeking unauthorized access to the weapons. In 1974, when Greece and Turkey went to war over Cyprus, American forces secretly removed all of NATO's nuclear weapons from Greece and cut the arming wires of the nuclear weapons stored in Turkey, rendering them useless.

overhead

Michael Walli wasn't the least bit contrite at the sentencing hearing. He quoted St Augustine's dictum that an unjust law is no law at all. 'I did no crime,' Walli told the court. 'I make no apology. I'm not remorseful. I have no sense of guilt or shame. I would do it again. I am the face of tomorrow, the face of total global demilitarization and the vindication of the prophets Isaiah and Micah.'

Gregory Boertje-Obed asked for permission to read a passage from 'Beyond Vietnam', a speech that Martin Luther King gave at Riverside Church in 1967. The permission was granted. In the speech, King had stressed the need for non-violent social change in the United States, while criticizing the behaviour of 'the greatest purveyor of violence in the world today – my own government'. Boertje-Obed offered to give a copy of the speech to Assistant US Attorney Theodore, who thanked him and accepted it. After reading some lines from a poem by Daniel Berrigan, Boertje-Obed expressed support for the Nuclear Non-Proliferation Treaty, hoping 'those nations that have nuclear weapons will negotiate in good faith to eliminate them completely at an early date'.

During the first part of the hearing, Mary Evelyn Tucker, a professor of world religions at Yale University, had testified that Sister Megan Rice was 'a person of high moral principles with a profound Christian commitment to alleviate suffering'. Tucker had known Sister Megan since childhood and asked the court not to impose a prison sentence on her dear friend. Sister Megan would have none of it. She thanked the judge, the prosecutors, and the defence attorneys. She criticized the military-industrial complex and talked about some of the inmates whom she'd recently met behind bars. 'To remain in prison for the rest of my life would be the greatest honour you could give me,' she said. 'Thank you. I hope it will happen.'

Sister Megan concluded her testimony by asking if she could lighten the atmosphere with a song. Judge Amul R. Thapar said that would be fine, and she led the courtroom in a brief rendition of 'Sacred the Land'.

'In our country, I firmly believe that breaking the law is not the answer,' Judge Thapar told the defendants, 'and I can't help think, as I listen to your allocutions, that if all that energy and passion was devoted to changing the laws, perhaps real change would have occurred by today.'

Thapar felt some regret at putting 'good people behind bars'. The sentences he imposed were about half as long as those sought by the prosecution. Sister Megan was given three years in prison, Walli and Boertje-Obed five.

The activists were also required to pay for the damage at Y-12. The cost to repair that damage was no longer the roughly $8,000 mentioned during the trial. The cost had somehow risen to $52,953. William P. Quigley, Walli's attorney, struggled to understand the huge discrepancy between those two sums. Babcock & Wilcox, the private contractor that operated Y-12, said that the $8,000 figure didn't include 'the incremental fringe rate', 'the burden labour rate' or 'the overhead' for getting the work done. Half a dozen painters had been brought to the uranium-storage facility on a Saturday, at a cost of more than $100 an hour each. Dog handlers, who had searched the site for intruders, had cost almost

$500 an hour. Videographers and photographers had been paid $7,000 to produce images of the graffiti and the torn chain link. Despite the large sums of money involved, the most expensive material that had to be bought to undo this act of sabotage was twenty five-gallon buckets of white paint.


pure and uncompromised

After considering the threat of nuclear terrorism for many years, William C. Potter, the director of the James Martin Center for Nonproliferation Studies, and Gary Ackerman, the director of the Unconventional Weapons and Technology Division, at the University of Maryland, outlined some of the motives that could drive a terrorist group to obtain a nuclear weapon. The group might hope to create mass anxiety or mass casualties. It might want to deter attacks by a state with nuclear weapons. It might want to destroy a large area belonging to an adversary. It might want the prestige that nuclear weapons seem to confer, the status of being a world power. And it might seek to fulfil a religious goal. Groups that have an apocalyptic outlook – that believe 'an irremediably corrupt world must be purged to make way for a utopian future', that celebrate violence as a means of achieving those aims – could be especially drawn to nuclear weapons, Potter and Ackerman found. Unfortunately, the number of those groups seems to be multiplying today.

'The ruling to kill Americans and their allies – civilians and military – is an individual duty for every Muslim who can do it in any country in which it is possible to do it,' Osama bin Laden declared in 1998. Bin Laden later met for three days with Chaudhry Abdul Majeed and Sultan Bashiruddin Mahmood, a couple of leading scientists in Pakistan's nuclear-weapons programme. There's conflicting evidence about whether Al Qaeda has ever seriously pursued the theft of a nuclear weapon or the construction of an improvised nuclear device. But the group's current leader, Ayman al-Zawahiri, has said that his mood won't improve until America vanishes. And he quoted, with approval, a radical imam's view that using a nuclear weapon against the United States would be sanctified by God: 'If a bomb were dropped on them, destroying ten million of them and burning as much of their land as they have burned of Muslim land, that would be permissible without any need to mention any other proof.'

The Salafi-jihadist world view promoted by Al

Qaeda holds that modern interpretations of the Quran are mistaken and deeply corrupted. 'Salaf' means 'ancestor', and Salafis believe one must live like the early followers of the Prophet Mohammed. They think their form of Islam is the only true one, pure and uncompromised. They have no tolerance for dissent or unbelievers. They don't consider jihad to be an internal, spiritual struggle. Salafis consider jihad a religious duty to purify corrupt states through violence, drive out infidels, and create a new caliphate – a perfect state in which religious and political leadership will be merged.

Seth G. Jones, the director of the International Security and Defense Policy Center at the RAND Corporation, estimates that there are about fifty Salafi-jihadist groups worldwide. They focus primarily on local struggles, battling the 'near enemy', not the 'far enemy': the United States. The groups most likely to commit terrorist acts on American soil are Al Qaeda, its offshoot Al Qaeda in the Arabian Peninsula, and the Islamic State in Iraq and al-Sham (ISIS). None have thus far engaged in nuclear terrorism, preferring more conventional and reliable forms of violence. But ISIS has gained notoriety lately by celebrating the slaughter of civilians and the destruction of cultural monuments, by crucifying and beheading its opponents, by proudly reducing churches and mosques to rubble. ISIS also celebrates committing suicide on behalf of jihad. A nuclear weapon could be the ideal means of salvation for someone with an eagerness to kill and a willingness to die for God.

Salafi jihadists aren't the only millenarian group that might be drawn to nuclear terrorism. During the early 1990s, the Japanese cult Aum Shinrikyo (Supreme Truth) attempted to buy nuclear weapons in Russia, purchased land in Australia to mine for uranium, and sought technical assistance from scientists at Moscow's leading institute for nuclear research. The leader of the cult, Shoko Asahara, was a partially blind yoga instructor who declared himself the reincarnation of both Jesus Christ and the Hindu god Shiva. Asahara thought his followers would be the only ones to survive the coming nuclear apocalypse. Unable to obtain nuclear weapons, members of Aum Shinrikyo developed chemical and biological weapons. In 1995, they launched an attack on the Tokyo subway system with sarin nerve gas that killed thirteen people and injured more than five thousand. Despite having about $1 billion in its bank account, perhaps fifty or sixty thousand followers worldwide, and the most advanced weapons-of-mass-destruction programme ever created by a terrorist group, the doomsday cult was unknown to Western intelligence agencies until the Tokyo subway attack.

White supremacists in the United States have also fantasized about using nuclear weapons to purify society. *The Turner Diaries* (1978), a novel long considered the bible of the white-power movement, features a protagonist who flies a plane carrying a nuclear weapon into the Pentagon, committing suicide in order to destroy Washington DC. His self-sacrifice is deemed heroic, the outcome of a sacred knowledge gained through much suffering: 'we are truly instruments of God in the fulfilment of his Grand Design'. Blacks, Jews, Asians, and Latinos aren't meant to survive that design.

In the concluding pages of *The Turner Diaries*, its 'happy' ending, white patriots use nuclear weapons stolen from Vandenberg Air Force Base, in California, to annihilate inferior races throughout the world.

Before Timothy McVeigh destroyed Oklahoma City's federal building with a truck bomb, in 1995, he travelled the country selling copies of *The Turner Diaries*. The book remains influential. The election of the first African-American president, the economic downturn, and resentment about illegal immigration have prompted an increase in white-power activism. Although the threat of Islamic terrorism has received a great deal of media attention, since 9/11 more people have been killed in the United States by American extremists than by foreign jihadists.

vulnerable and exposed

When I visited the Y-12 National Security Complex a few months ago, the place looked like an odd mix of Silicon Valley and the industrial ruins of Detroit. The site has a handful of modern shiny new buildings, some of the most advanced and precise machine tools in the world, capable of accurately fabricating uranium to within millionths of an inch – and an abandoned steam plant in the middle of the complex, rusting and decayed, with grass growing in the cracks of surrounding pavement. Buildings and equipment dating back to the Manhattan Project are still in use. Inside one building, I saw calutrons – enormous contraptions, about fifteen feet high, relying on powerful magnets to enrich uranium – that were designed more than seventy years ago, and which are still kept on standby to produce stable isotopes, if necessary. A dusty basement was filled with spare parts, gauges, huge vacuum tubes, unopened spools of cable marked with their original date of manufacture

(1944). The room felt like an exhibit at a museum of technology, a steampunk fantasy.

Inside the Protected Area, the security was impressive. Large coils of razor wire have been placed between fences to slow anyone trying to cut through them. I saw security guards with automatic weapons, plenty of video cameras, barriers to prevent car bombs and truck bombs. The Highly Enriched Uranium Materials Facility appears massive and intimidating. I have been told that if an intruder somehow managed to get inside, he or she would confront a series of lethal impediments before getting anywhere near the uranium.

Wackenhut is no longer responsible for the security at Y-12. Two months after the break-in, its contract was terminated, and Babcock & Wilcox took over the guard force. Creating a single, integrated management structure at the site promised to improve its security. But a couple of embarrassing incidents soon occurred. On 6 June 2013, Brenda L. Haptonstall, a sixty-two-year-old woman, was allowed to pass through the main entrance at Y-12 and drive the full length of the complex without being asked to show any identification. Haptonstall later said that she had been looking for a low-cost apartment building that she'd spotted in an ad. The sight of 'nice officers waving her through with illuminated flashlight cones' didn't strike her as unusual, according to the police report. There's probably been an accident, she thought, driving into the high-security nuclear-weapons site. The following month, on the first anniversary of the Plowshares action at Y-12, a security guard accidentally fired his gun inside an armoured vehicle. Fragments ricocheting off the interior armour injured him and another guard. Babcock & Wilcox's contract at Y-12 was not renewed.

Consolidated Nuclear Security (CNS), a consortium headed by Bechtel and Lockheed Martin, has operated Y-12 since last July. CNS is in charge of the security equipment and the security personnel at the site. Although the guard force there is largely unchanged, new managers run it. Morgan Smith, the chief operating officer of CNS, seems tough, competent, and blunt. He previously ran the Knolls Atomic Power Laboratory, a Bechtel facility north of Albany, New York, that helps maintain nuclear reactors for the US Navy. Smith makes no excuses for the security lapses at Y-12 that preceded his arrival. 'What happened in 2012 became something that could be used, going forward, in a very positive way across the complex,' he says. All the employees at the site are now expected to feel personally responsible for its security. Smith feels confident that Y-12 is a more secure place today than in the past. And he says that the guards want 'to do everything possible to restore the pride and reputation' of their force.

Standing atop Chestnut Ridge with my hosts and a security contingent, looking down at the Y-12 complex, I instinctively felt uneasy. The valley that the site occupies is quite narrow, the hills overlooking it densely wooded. The fear of a sniper that had made Sergeant Riggs put on body armour before dealing with the Plowshares intruders suddenly made sense. Terrorists attacking Y-12 from the ridge would have the advantage of high ground and a great deal of cover. At night, they would be hard to see. Ideally, some of the trees on those hills would be chopped down for security reasons, regardless of what local environmentalists might think. From the ridge top, America's most important storage facility for weapons-grade uranium no longer looked so intimidating. It looked vulnerable and exposed. During the Middle Ages, castles were built at the top of a hill, not at the bottom.

Weeks later, I learned that others had expressed similar concerns about Y-12 for years. The initial design of the Highly Enriched Uranium Materials Facility was a concrete bunker covered on top and

on three sides by an earthen berm. When Babcock & Wilcox assumed management of Y-12, in
2000, it changed the design, claiming that a building above ground would be less expensive. Four
years later, the Department of Energy's Inspector
General argued that an above-ground, fortress-like
design would actually be more expensive and less
secure. Danielle Brian, the head of the Project on
Government Oversight, stressed those very points
during Congressional testimony in May 2004. An
above-ground storage facility would have five
exposed surfaces – four walls and a roof – that terrorists could attack. A bermed facility would have
only one.

Babcock & Wilcox nevertheless proceeded to
build the facility above ground, the big white
castle, with its four turrets and walls. Originally
estimated to cost taxpayers about $253 million,
the Highly Enriched Uranium Materials Facility
wound up costing more than twice that amount.
And because it's not underground, it needs more
officers to guard its perimeter. The most secure
nuclear-weapons-storage site in the United States,
according to the military and civilian experts whom
I consulted, is the Kirtland Underground Munitions
Storage Complex at Kirtland Air Force Base, in Albu-
querque, New Mexico. In satellite photographs,

aside from an entrance ramp and an exit ramp, the structure is practically invisible.

After the break-in at Y-12, Wackenhut also lost the contract to provide security at the neighbouring Oak Ridge National Laboratory. But today Wackenhut is still the security contractor at the Savannah River Site, outside Aiken, South Carolina – where about 20,000 pounds of plutonium are stored. Savannah River is a difficult site to protect. It extends across 200,000 acres, and a state highway cuts through the middle of it. In late 2012, Wackenhut received a bonus for its 'exceptional level of performance' at the site. The following January, Wackenhut failed a Department of Energy security test at Savannah River, allowing commandos to seize fissile materials in a mock attack. A representative of Wackenhut – now owned by a private equity firm and renamed the Centerra Group – later emphasized that the overall security audit had a 'satisfactory outcome'.

A company called National Strategic Protective Services (NSPS) won the $182 million contract to replace Wackenhut at the Oak Ridge laboratory, where some weapons-grade uranium is kept. NSPS is a joint venture formed by two large security companies. One of them, Triple Canopy, has for years provided security at American embassies and bases in Iraq. The Department of Justice alleged in 2012 that 'Triple Canopy knowingly billed the United States for hundreds of foreign nationals it hired as security guards who could not meet fire-arms proficiency tests established by the army and required under the contract'. The company had recruited guards in Uganda and brought them to Iraq. Many of the guards did not know how to fire their assault rifles accurately or safely – a skill necessary for protecting Al Asad Air Base, a crucial American base during the Iraq war. The Justice Department also claimed that Triple Canopy's managers in Iraq repeatedly falsified test scorecards to cover up the guards' lack of proficiency – and that high-level executives at the company were aware of the fraud. 'For a government contractor to knowingly provide deficient security services, as is alleged in this case, is unthinkable, especially in war time,' said a Justice Department official. The case is still pending in court.

Triple Canopy was bought last year by the Constellis Group, a conglomerate that has taken over a number of large security firms. One of them, Academi, used to do business under a different name: Blackwater.

The Y-12 National Security Complex may be known as the Fort Knox of Uranium, but the United

States Bullion Depository, the real Fort Knox, in Kentucky, is guarded by federal officers. They are members of the US Mint Police, a law-enforcement agency that's been in continuous operation since 1792. Their first loyalty is to the United States, not a multinational corporation. And Fort Knox is right next door to Fort Knox, an army base with thousands of soldiers. Nobody has ever broken into the bullion depositary, and none of its roughly 4,500 tons of gold have ever been stolen. The Federal Reserve Bank of New York has 7,000 tons of gold in its vaults. The gold is stored deeply underground in Lower Manhattan and guarded by members of the US Federal Reserve Police. As the name implies, they are also federal employees. The location of the Federal Reserve's gold vaults isn't top secret. Tens of thousands of tourists visit them every year, and yet nobody has thus far returned to Liberty Street in the middle of the night and snuck back into the vaults.

A pound of gold is worth about $20,000. A pound of weapons-grade uranium, on the black market, could be worth at least a hundred times that amount. Logic would dictate that the more valuable commodity should be guarded more securely. And yet the laws of free enterprise have not been fully applied to America's nuclear enterprise.

The financial liability of the private contractors at nuclear-weapons sites is strictly limited by the Price-Anderson Nuclear Industries Indemnity Act. If terrorists manage to steal weapons-grade uranium or plutonium from a Department of Energy facility because of a contractor's mistakes, the firm responsible for the security breach stands to lose its contract. The United States could lose a city.

threat reduction

Sam Nunn was in Budapest when a group of hard-line Communists detained Mikhail Gorbachev, the president of the Soviet Union, and attempted to seize power. Nunn worried about who was in control of the Soviet nuclear arsenal. It was the third week of August in 1991. He was a Democratic senator from Georgia, a prominent member of the Armed Services Committee, and he'd long been worried about the theft or misuse of a nuclear weapon. During the 1980s, while others warned about the threat of a Soviet surprise attack, Nunn had come to believe that the risk of an accident, a terrorist act, or a foul-up with a nuclear weapon was a lot greater. A few days after the coup attempt in the Soviet Union failed, he flew to Moscow and saw the large crowds of demonstrators in the streets. Nunn got the sense that an empire was collapsing, that things were spiralling out of control. And that empire had about 30,000 nuclear weapons.

At first, Nunn's fears were dismissed by the White House and other members of Congress. But as the Soviet Union began to come apart, a realization soon dawned: not only nuclear weapons but also biological and chemical weapons would be scattered throughout its former territory, without oversight from any clear, centralized authority. The world's largest stockpile of plutonium and weapons-grade uranium would also be up for grabs. And then something that today seems almost unimaginable happened. Democrats and Republicans in Congress worked closely together and passed legislation to foster greater cooperation between the Russia and the United States. Drafted by Nunn and Richard Lugar, a Republican senator from Indiana, the Soviet Threat Reduction Act became law on 12 December 1991. Two weeks later, the Soviet Union no longer existed.

The Nunn-Lugar Cooperative Threat Reduction Program sought to dismantle weapons of mass destruction in the former Soviet republics, secure fissile materials, and prevent nuclear terrorism. In the early 1990s, the situation was dire. Thousands of nuclear weapons had to be withdrawn from the field and safely locked away. The weapons could be stolen where they were deployed, during shipment, even at the main Russian storage sites, which often had rudimentary security systems. Hundreds of tons of fissile materials were even more vulnerable to theft. The Soviet Union had never conducted an inventory of its plutonium and weapons-grade uranium. Nobody knew how much there was, let alone whether any of it was missing. Nunn visited a Russian nuclear site where buckets of highly enriched uranium were being stored in an unguarded warehouse with broken windows.

The insider threat caused the greatest concern. Once among the elite of Soviet society, nuclear scientists and engineers were now struggling to get paid. The head of Chelyabinsk-70, one of the two 'closed cities' in the Soviet Union devoted to nuclear-weapon research, committed suicide, overwhelmed by his inability to take care of its employees. At a laboratory south of Moscow, a nuclear engineer named Leonid Smirnov stole small vials of weapons-grade uranium for months, hoping to sell it. He was caught inadvertently. While standing at a train station, Smirnov bumped into some neighbours. The neighbours were drunk and soon attracted the attention of police – who arrested all of them. When the police searched Smirnov's bag, they were startled to find lead canisters filled with weapons-grade uranium.

The Nunn-Lugar programme was an extraordinary success, strongly supported by Democratic and Republican presidents for more than two decades. It helped to remove nuclear weapons and fissile materials from Belarus, Kazakhstan, and Ukraine; consolidate weapon storage at a smaller number of sites in Russia; upgrade the security at those sites; and construct the Mayak Fissile Material Storage Facility, an immense, fortified warehouse that now stores thousands of nuclear warheads, as well as plutonium and weapons-grade uranium. More importantly, the Nunn-Lugar programme encouraged close collaboration between the scientific and military elite of two former enemies. The fact that no nuclear weapons went missing, amid the chaos following the Soviet Union's collapse, can be attributed not only to the assistance provided by Nunn-Lugar but also to the patriotism of Russian officers and scientists. They could have earned a fortune by selling a nuclear weapon and, as far as we know, didn't.

Nunn-Lugar's achievements now have a certain poignancy. In December 2014, Congress voted to cut funding for it. And Russia announced that it would end most of its cooperative work with the United States, despite the need to upgrade security at more than 200 buildings. After leaving the Senate, Sam Nunn helped to found the Nuclear Threat Initiative, a non-profit dedicated to reducing the danger posed by weapons of mass destruction. He's often described the effort to prevent nuclear terrorism as 'a race between cooperation and catastrophe'. The Russian decision to stop collaborating on nuclear issues, Nunn thinks, just made the latter more likely.

it hasn't, it won't

On 5 April 2009, standing before tens of thousands of people in Prague's central square, President Barack Obama gave his first major foreign-policy speech. His call for 'a world without nuclear weapons' was widely reported. But Obama also addressed the prospect of nuclear terrorism, describing it as 'the most immediate and extreme threat to global security'. He promised to lead an international effort that would safeguard all of the world's vulnerable fissile materials within four years. To fulfil that promise and reduce the risk of nuclear terrorism, Obama hosted world leaders at a summit in Washington DC, in 2010. Two more nuclear-security summits have been held since then, one in Seoul, the other at The Hague. Some progress on the issue has been made. A dozen countries have completely eliminated their stocks of high-risk fissile material, and Japan agreed to get rid of more than a thousand pounds of weapons-grade uranium and plutonium. Much more remains to be done, however. Japan still has close to 20,000 pounds of plutonium. International standards have been set for how to run nuclear reactors but not for how to secure the dangerous fissile materials that those reactors produce. And Russia has announced it will not attend the 2016 Nuclear Security Summit in Chicago.

The momentum to prevent nuclear terrorism has slowed in the United States, as well. The bitterness in Congress, the lack of cooperation, and the budget sequestration have been responsible for large reductions in spending on nuclear-security programmes. The amount of money that will be saved this year by cutting these programmes – about $340 million – is equivalent to 0.06 per cent of the 2015 defence budget. These short-term savings could prove to be expensive in the long run.

The number of nuclear weapons has declined precipitously since the end of the Cold War, and the physical security of nuclear materials has been much improved. The fact that an act of nuclear terrorism has not yet occurred may be due to the complexity of mounting such an attack, the effectiveness of counterterrorist efforts, a fear of the potential backlash, or a general lack of interest among terrorist groups that might have the capability to commit one. But the fact that it hasn't happened does not mean it won't. There are still about 16,000 nuclear weapons in the world. Terrorists only need to steal one. And there's about three million pounds of weapons-grade uranium, as well as about a million pounds of plutonium, stored at hundreds of different locations. As long as these fissile materials exist somewhere, so will the threat that a terrorist might get hold of them. An improvised nuclear device with one-fifteenth the explosive force of the Hiroshima bomb, detonated at a certain time, at a certain urban location in the United States, could kill about 200,000 people. A nuclear device with two-thirds the explosive force of the Hiroshima bomb, detonated at a certain American port, could kill about 60,000 people, force the evacuation of about six million, and cause about $1 trillion worth of property damage.

The loss of life and economic harm caused by a single nuclear detonation in the United States would cause profound social and political changes. Having destroyed one city, a terrorist group could claim to have other nuclear devices hidden in other cities. The restrictions on civil liberties that followed 9/11 will seem trivial compared to those likely to be adopted after an act of nuclear terrorism. Last year marked the tenth anniversary of the 9/11 Commission Report, which tried to explain how nineteen men armed only with knives and box cutters destroyed two of the largest, most iconic buildings in the United States. I recently asked Lee H. Hamilton, a co-chairman of the 9/11 Commission, whether the threat of nuclear terrorism has been exaggerated. Hamilton is a former chairman of the House Intelligence Committee, with the manner of a solid and sober Midwesterner. He thinks acts of nuclear terrorism are the greatest national-security threat that America faces today. And he cannot understand the complacency in Washington. 'I don't get any sense of urgency about nuclear terrorism,' Hamilton said. 'What the hell are we doing, that's the question I keep asking.'

the road to abolition

This summer will mark the seventieth anniversary of the atomic bomb's invention and its use against two Japanese cities. The anniversary will be commemorated by rallies and speeches demanding the abolition of nuclear weapons. That has been the professed desire of most American presidents since 1945, including Harry Truman. But I've spoken with military officers, academics, and former Pentagon officials who think the notion of abolishing nuclear weapons is a dangerous and impossible fantasy. They would like the United States to modernize its nuclear weapons and delivery systems instead. Their arguments go something like this:

Fifty to sixty million people were killed during the Second World War. America's nuclear weapons not only ended that war but also played a critical role in avoiding a third one. Indeed, our nuclear weapons prevented the Soviet domination of Japan and Western Europe. History has shown that traditional enemies who have nuclear weapons don't fight wars against one another. Nuclear deterrence works. Both China and Russia are now spending heavily to modernize their nuclear forces. If the United States doesn't modernize as well, it will appear weak. It will become an inferior nuclear power. And if the United States unilaterally reduces the number of weapons in its arsenal, allies currently shielded under its 'nuclear umbrella', like Japan and South Korea, will build their own nuclear weapons – greatly increasing the likelihood of a nuclear war. Tampering with a national-security strategy that has kept the peace among world powers for seventy years would be a risky and irrational move. A treaty to abolish nuclear weapons would be as effective as the Kellogg-Briand Pact, an international agreement, signed by the United States in 1928, that outlawed war.

The Catholic Church once agreed with many of those arguments. For most of the Cold War, the Vatican was staunchly anti-Communist, and nuclear deterrence was blessed as a means of containing the influence of the Soviet Union. In keeping with the Geneva Convention, the targeting of civilians and the indiscriminate destruction of cities was condemned by the Church. But at least one American bishop suggested that low-yield nuclear weapons could be used morally 'against military objectives in a just war according to theological principles'. Dorothy Day's pacifism was outside of the Catholic mainstream, and she was constantly at odds with Francis Cardinal Spellman, the Archbishop of New York. Spellman thought the American troops in Vietnam were 'soldiers of Christ' who were fighting a 'war for civilization'. In 1982, Pope John Paul shifted the church's position on nuclear weapons, declaring that deterrence was 'morally acceptable' only if it served as 'a step on the way toward a progressive disarmament'. When the Cold War ended, the reliance on nuclear weapons to maintain world peace became harder to justify.

Last December, the Vatican released a statement that broke from decades of Church teaching on nuclear weapons. The distinction between having them and using them seems to have vanished. 'Now is the time to affirm not only the immorality of nuclear weapons, but the immorality of their possession, thereby clearing the road to abolition,' the Vatican said. And Dorothy Day, once mocked and reviled, is now being promoted for sainthood by Cardinal Timothy M. Dolan, the conservative Archbishop of New York.

a prophet and a saint

The Department of Justice doesn't seem proud of having imprisoned the Plowshares activists who broke into Y-12. Nobody at the Justice Department or the US Attorney's Office in Knoxville would discuss the case with me. Nor would the two prosecutors who handled the case.

Sister Megan Rice is currently imprisoned at the Metropolitan Detention Center in Brooklyn. My request to visit her was denied by Kimberly Ask-Carlson, the prison's warden. When I appealed the decision, my request was denied again. Asked for an explanation, Warden Ask-Carlson wrote me a letter that said, 'I have decided to deny your request due to safety and security concerns.' When I inquired whose safety and security might be jeopardized by my visit, a prison spokesman declined to answer. Sister Megan is eighty-five, one of the oldest women in the federal prison system, and she has a heart condition. During roughly the same period in which the Justice Department refused to let me meet with her for security reasons, the NNSA allowed me to visit three high-security nuclear-weapons sites.

I corresponded with Sister Megan for months, and she was eventually allowed to speak to me on the phone for an hour. We talked about her upbringing in Manhattan, her parents, and their commitment to racial equality in the 1930s. She told me about her years in Africa and her introduction to the peace movement. We discussed what happened at Y-12. But the subject that Sister Megan now seems the most passionate about is the suffering of her fellow inmates. She is confined in a dormitory, not a cell. It has about sixty bunk beds, separated from one another by a few feet, without any partitions. There is no privacy, and the room can get 'shrieking' loud. Many of the women seem to have been incarcerated for drug offences. She thinks that most of them have been the victims of abuse. Instead of complaining or focusing on her own case, she has encouraged inmates to write to me about theirs. At the end of a conversation that felt too brief, Sister Megan said, 'Bless you, brother. And thanks.'

Michael Walli is being held at the Federal Correctional Institution, McKean, a medium-security facility in north-west Pennsylvania. I wasn't allowed to visit him, either, for reasons that were never specified. We were, however, permitted to speak on the phone. And I got a strong sense of Walli's personality, without having to be in the same room. His recall of dates and numbers is extraordinary, and, despite being a high-school dropout, he readily quotes passages of the Bible and lines from Martin Luther King's speeches. Walli believes that King is literally a saint, despite having been a Baptist, and considers Sister Megan to be a prophet of God. When I asked about the sabotage charge, Walli let loose. 'Well, the US Government has trespassed against its own constitutional, legal obligations by its torture policies, its assassination campaigns, its illegal wars, a whole bunch of illegal weapons besides the nuclear weapons,' he said. 'The US Government is a failed, rogue, terrorist nation.'

As for the Y-12 break-in, Walli thinks it would have received more media coverage if they'd been shot. And he was prepared for that to happen. 'I'm ready to go into the afterlife,' Walli said. 'My citizenship is in heaven. When I go off into the judgement seat before Jesus Christ, the just judge, I'm not going to wave a US flag in Jesus's face, that's for sure.' He will be sixty-nine years old when he's released.


at any moment


I've visited dozens of prisons over the past twenty years, and Leavenworth Penitentiary remains the most unsettling. It was the first prison I'd ever been to, and I went there to see a hippie biker who'd been given a life sentence, without parole, for a non-violent marijuana crime. The federal prosecutor in the case hadn't really wanted to seek a life sentence. But when the hippie biker refused to testify against others, that's what he got. At the time, Leavenworth was not only the oldest prison in the federal system but also one of the most dangerous. It was a maximum-security facility built in 1903 and

crammed with bank robbers, killers, even terrorists. The hippie biker seemed out of place. And the
architecture of the prison appeared just as surreal
to me as the punishment for that relatively minor
pot crime. Leavenworth was designed to look like
the US Capitol building in Washington DC. Imagine
the Capitol, flattened, stretched, and surrounded by
forty-foot-high walls made of red brick and topped
with gun towers. As I headed up the steep concrete
steps again, this time to see Gregory Boertje-Obed,
I thought about the thousands of violent inmates
who'd been locked away there. Many had reached
the top of the stairs, walked into the place, and
never walked out.

I met Boertje-Obed in a small visiting room filled
with beige plastic chairs. The only other people in
the room were a prison official and a corrections
officer, both of them polite and friendly and not
especially interested in our conversation. Leavenworth is a medium-security facility today. But gang
members and murderers are still incarcerated
there, amid a prison culture rigidly divided by race.
The typical inmate is serving a ten-year sentence.
In an environment that would frighten most
people, Boertje-Obed seemed calm, grounded, and
philosophical. He was there for a reason, and just
fine with it.

As a young man, Boertje-Obed seemed an unlikely candidate for a cell block in Leavenworth Penitentiary. He grew up in a series of Iowa towns – Pella, Sioux Center, Ames. His father was a biology teacher, and the family was deeply religious. For a while, they attended two services at the local Dutch Reformed church every Sunday. Boertje-Obed went to Tulane University in 1973, joined the army Reserve Officers Training Corps to help cover the tuition, and then entered a graduate programme at Louisiana State University to study social psychology. He wrote a master's thesis on whether personality tests could predict leadership ability and hoped to become an academic researcher. Before that could happen, he became a first lieutenant in the army to fulfil his ROTC obligations.

Assigned to a combat-engineer battalion at Fort Polk, in central Louisiana, Boertje-Obed trained to be a supervisor at a medical-aid station. In battle, his job would be to organize the care of the wounded. In 1980, he was part of a major field exercise in Louisiana. During the war game, a Soviet armoured column headed south from Monroe toward his unit. His battalion camped out in the fields and prepared for a nuclear, biological, or chemical attack, donning gas masks and protective suits. Boertje-Obed was in charge of the medics. He had to make sure that everyone wore the masks for an hour, then two hours, then three, four, five. Members of his unit began to cheat, pulling the masks away from their faces. It was excruciating to wear the masks for ten minutes, let alone four or five hours. The whole exercise seemed pointless to Boertje-Obed; he would die during a real attack.

Boertje-Obed had begun reading about Dorothy Day, who'd encouraged workers at munitions plants to walk away from their jobs. 'God will lead and provide for you,' she had assured them. It seemed as though Day were speaking directly to him. He read the Bible and books about civil disobedience. He started to believe you should love your enemies. The field exercise was his tipping point. 'Nope,' he thought. 'I won't cooperate any more in the planning for nuclear war.'

The captain of Boertje-Obed's unit sent him to see the colonel who commanded the battalion. The colonel had served in Vietnam. He listened carefully to Boertje-Obed and agreed that wearing the mask for hours was impractical. The colonel said that the leaders of the United States and the Soviet Union should be forced to wear those masks – it would make them seek peace. Instead of trying to talk Boertje-Obed out of quitting the army, he explained the procedures for becoming a conscientious objector.

Boertje-Obed left the army, returned to Baton Rouge, and took theology classes at LSU. He became involved in anti-nuclear activism, studied non-violent resistance with Daniel Berrigan, moved to Jonah House, and lived there for seventeen years. Boertje-Obed and Philip Berrigan painted houses together three or four times a week and planned break-ins at nuclear-weapons sites. Boertje-Obed's life became a series of protests, arrests, jailings, and imprisonments on behalf of peace. At one point, like the Berrigans, he went on the run. But that was an exception. On a fundamental level, he accepted responsibility for his actions. When a court-appointed attorney tried to persuade a jury that he was innocent during a Plowshares trial, pointing to the absence of fingerprints or photographs linking him to the scene, Boertje-Obed stood up, told the jury he'd done it, and started to explain why. The judge cited him for contempt of court.

In the months leading up to the Y-12 break-in, Boertje-Obed was happily married, living at the Loaves and Fishes Catholic Worker House in Duluth, and painting houses. One of the few times that he cross-examined a government witness during the trial in Knoxville was to question the amount of paint that Babcock & Wilcox bought to cover up the graffiti. He thought a hundred gallons sounded excessive.

One of Boertje-Obed's favourite books was introduced as evidence by the prosecutors. He'd brought a copy of it into the Protected Area at Y-12. *Christian Idolatry/Christian Revival* (1993) was written by a friend of his, Kurt Greenhalgh. The book criticizes the sinfulness and corruption of most contemporary churches, the wide gulf between their practices and Christ's teachings. And it warns Christians not to obey the militaristic, idolatrous, man-made laws of the nation state: 'History is not kind to those who exalt themselves.'

Boertje-Obed was slight and soft-spoken, wearing a beige prison uniform that looked a couple of sizes too big. But, as I listened to him talk about his faith and his devotion to non-violence, it became clear that deep down he was harder and tougher than most of the inmates in the yard. Henry David Thoreau spent a single night in jail as an act of civil disobedience and then wrote a famous essay about it. Boertje-Obed had already spent more than a thousand nights behind bars for his beliefs and may spend at least a thousand more. He seemed to have no regrets. 'You must live your Christian beliefs fully,' he told me, 'as though judgement may come at any moment.'

Boertje-Obed said that no one from the government has ever asked him for suggestions about how the security at nuclear-weapons sites could be improved. He certainly doesn't want terrorists to do what he's done. The Bureau of Prisons sent him to Leavenworth, nine hours away from his family, he said, because it considers him to be a 'domestic terrorist'. Boertje-Obed plays a lot of Scrabble now, belongs to a Bible-study group, and spends time teaching someone in his cell block how to read. If Boertje-Obed's attacked by another inmate, he won't fight back. But he might intervene to separate other inmates who are fighting.

Right before the corrections officer led him out of the room, Boertje-Obed looked me in eye and gave a subtle little smile.

I stood across the street from Leavenworth Penitentiary for a moment, taking in the view. When I'd visited the place twenty years ago, the sky was gloomy and grey. Now it was clear and blue. Sunshine glistened in the razor wire, and the Stars and Stripes hung from a flagpole in front of the steps. The prison looked like an image on an old postcard, a haunting, uniquely American symbol of state power. And a thought occurred to me: the walls of the penitentiary guarding this pacifist were taller and more impenetrable than any of the fences at Y-12.

*9 March 2015*

# Acknowledgements

I'm grateful to the following Plowshares activists for speaking to me about their life's work: Michael Walli, Sister Megan Rice, Gregory Boertje-Obed, Liz McAllister, Sister Ardeth Platte, Sister Carol Gilbert, John LaForge, Father Steven Kelly, Father Carl Kabat, and Father William 'Bix' Bichsel. Father Bix passed away in February 2015, at the age of eighty-six – a few months after joining a protest on Jeju Island, in South Korea, against the construction of a new military base.

I'm also grateful to the officials at the National Nuclear Security Administration and Consolidated Nuclear Security who spoke with me on the record and facilitated my visit to the Y-12 National Security Complex: Steven Erhart, Morgan Smith, Ray Smith, and Steven Wyatt. They do not want another security lapse at Y-12 ever to occur again.

I spoke off the record to a number of anti-nuclear activists, government officials, and retired military personnel with nuclear expertise. They know who they are, and their help was invaluable.

Frank Munger, a senior writer at the *Knoxville News Sentinel*, has covered the news from Y-12 for more than three decades. His reporting on the break-in and its aftermath was terrific. I'm grateful to Munger for taking me to the Scarboro Church of Christ and showing me the route that the Plowshares activists followed up Pine Ridge. The fact that the two of us were confronted, just moments after stepping onto the path, by a pair of angry church ladies reassured me about the new security measures at Y-12. With great moral authority, the women asked us to leave the property immediately – and we did.

One of the attorneys in the Plowshares case, William P. Quigley, helped me to understand not only the trial but also the legal predicament of everyone who now engages in civil disobedience. Two other defence attorneys, Judy Kwan and Marc R. Shapiro, provided me with court transcripts and details about the ongoing appeal. And Mary Evelyn Tucker, a senior lecturer and senior research scholar at the Yale School of Forestry & Environmental Studies, shared her recollections of the sentencing hearing and her family's long friendship with Sister Megan.

I'm grateful to Warden Claude Maye and Treavor Kroger at Leavenworth Penitentiary for letting me spend time with Gregory Boertje-Obed. In a free society, being imprisoned should never lead to being silenced.

I first learned about the break-in at Y-12 while visiting the World Institute for Nuclear Security (WINS) in Vienna. WINS is a non-governmental organization dedicated to preventing the theft, diversion, or misuse of fissile and radioactive materials. Its executive director, Dr Roger Howsley, and its Academy Manager, Daniel Johnson, introduced me to many of the nuclear-security challenges now faced by governments throughout the world.

At the Nuclear Threat Initiative (NTI), Des Browne, Cathy Gwin, Corey Hinderstein, Carmen MacDougall, Joan Rohlfing, Deborah G. Rosenblum, and Dr Page Stoutland taught me a great deal about the dangers still posed by weapons of mass destruction. I'm especially grateful to Sam Nunn, the chief executive officer of NTI, for his time and his help. Nunn has probably done more than any other single person to reduce the risk of nuclear terrorism. He deserves a lot more recognition, and a few more medals, for that work.

Danielle Brian, the executive director of the Project on Government Oversight, and Peter Stockton, the group's principal investigator, have been warning for years about the mismanagement of American nuclear facilities. Their analysis of the problem and the documents that they've obtained were extremely useful.

I benefited enormously from reading the work of academics experts on nuclear terrorism and from discussing the subject with them. Matthew Bunn is a professor of practice at Harvard University's John F. Kennedy School of Government and co-principal investigator of its Project on Managing the Atom. At Harvard, at the National Academy of Sciences, and in government, Bunn has played a leading role in the effort to ensure that nuclear weapons and fissile materials are never stolen. Scott D. Sagan, a professor of political science at Stanford University, has a unique grasp of both nuclear-security and nuclear-command-and-control issues. Siegfried S. Hecker, a former director of the Los Alamos National Laboratory and a professor in the department of management science and engineering at Stanford, spoke to me about some of the technical aspects of securing nuclear material and the importance of continuing to work closely with Russian nuclear scientists. William C. Potter, director of the James Martin Center for Nonproliferation Studies at the Monterey Institute of International Studies, is a leading expert on nuclear terrorism, non-proliferation, and the national-security policies of contemporary Russia. I am grateful for his help with those issues.

I learned much about the threat of Salafi-jihadist terrorism and weapons of mass destruction from Gary Ackerman, the director of the Unconventional Weapons and Technology Division, at the University of Maryland; Seth G. Jones, the director of the International Security and Defense Policy Center at the RAND Corporation; Anne Stenersen, a research fellow at the Norwegian Defense Research Establishment; and from the writings of Rolf Mowatt-Larssen, a senior fellow at Harvard University's Belfer Center for Science and International Affairs. I'm not sure how they sleep at night.

For the past seven years, I've had two remarkable mentors in all things nuclear: Sidney Drell, a professor and deputy director emeritus of the SLAC National Accelerator Laboratory, Stanford University, and Bob Peurifoy, a former vice president and director of weapons development at the Sandia National Laboratories. Their views about nuclear terrorism helped to form mine. It's hard to imagine public servants with a greater concern for the public interest. Any mistakes in these pages are entirely my own.

This book began during a long conversation about prisons and nuclear weapons with David Remnick, the editor of the *New Yorker*. I somehow managed to write something that combined both of my long-standing interests. Remnick was extraordinarily patient and supportive from the first day until the last, despite how many months stretched in between. His magazine is one of the last great supporters of long-form investigative journalism. And the *New Yorker* has published some of the greatest writing on the nuclear threat. It was a real privilege to find my work in the same magazine that commissioned John Hersey's 'Hiroshima', John McPhee's 'The Curve of Binding Energy', and Jonathan Schell's 'The Fate of the Earth'. Those three classics are still powerful, disturbing and, unfortunately, relevant today.

At the *New Yorker*, John Bennet did a wonderful job of encouraging and editing me. Carolyn Kormann did most of the fact-checking, with assistance from Clare Malone and Neima Jahromi. Some of these details were not easy to confirm. I am deeply grateful for, and humbled by, every error they found. And Betsy Morais helped me with all the logistics.

At Penguin, Stefan McGrath has proven once again to be a bold editor and a dear friend.

Tina Bennett, my literary agent, is simply the best.

And without Red, my antidote to the darkness, this book would never have been written.

# A Note on Sources

Those wishing to know more about Catholic pacifism and the Plowshares movement will find much to enjoy in the memoirs of its three seminal figures: Dorothy Day's *The Long Loneliness: The Autobiography of the Legendary Catholic Social Activist* (New York: HarperOne, 2009); Philip Berrigan's *Fighting the Lamb's War: Skirmishes with the American Empire* (Bloomington, Ind.: iUniverse, 2011); and Daniel Berrigan's *To Dwell in Peace: An Autobiography* (San Francisco: Harper & Row, 1987).

I also recommend *Dorothy Day: A Radical Devotion*, by Robert Coles (New York: Da Capo Press, 1987). Rosalie G. Riegle has compiled two fine volumes of oral history about American pacifism: *Crossing the Line: Nonviolent Resisters Speak Out for Peace* (Eugene, Oreg.: Cascade Books, 2013) and *Doing Time for Peace: Resistance, Family, and Community* (Nashville, Tenn.: Vanderbilt University Press, 2013). For a broader historical perspective, I suggest Dan McKanan's *Prophetic Encounters: Religion and the American Radical Tradition* (Boston: Beacon Press, 2011).

My previous books have included extensive source notes. The text of this book contains all that I'd like to reveal about the threat of nuclear terrorism. Readers seeking additional information about it should look elsewhere.

# Postscript

On 8 May 2015, the sabotage convictions of Michael Walli, Sister Megan Rice, and Gregory Boertje-Obed were overturned by a three-judge panel of the US Court of Appeals for the Sixth Circuit. Raymond Kethledge, the judge who wrote the opinion, was appointed to the court by President George W. Bush. 'The defendants' actions in this case had zero effect, at the time of their actions or any time afterwards, on the nation's ability to wage war or defend against attack,' the opinion said. Instead of proving that sabotage had been committed and America's security endangered, the prosecutors had offered only 'vague platitudes.'

One of the defense attorneys, William P. Quigley, was surprised by the ruling. This was the first time in thirty years that the sabotage conviction of a Plowshares activist had been overturned. Quigley thought the decision conveyed a strong message to federal judges: 'Peaceful protest isn't sabotage.'

A week later, in a highly unusual move, the court of appeals ordered that Walli, Sister Megan, and

Boertje-Obed be released from prison immediately. The court thought it likely that they had already served more time than was warranted by the conviction for destroying government property. They walked free on 16 May 2015. And Sister Megan, no longer silenced by prison authorities, gave a series of television interviews.

As of this writing, the government has not yet decided whether to challenge the court's ruling on the sabotage charge. The three Plowshares activists are still obligated to pay a $52,953 fine for the break-in at Y-12. But they have neither the means nor the intention of paying it.